AC[

"Breathe has all the makings of the perfect story-- lies, acceptance, deception, anger, tragedy, rejection and triumph. It captures the pure essence of every black, gay man's life at some point or another. And after you read it, you'll truly want to breathe!"
--Trent Jackson, Author of *At This Moment*

"Blair writes with a passion and verve reminiscent of James Earl Hardy. This story is told the way so many in society are living it. Breathe will have you turning the pages anxious to know what happens next."
--Anna J., *Essence* **Bestselling Author of** *My Woman His Wife*

"Blair has written a gripping novella that seethes with the youthful angst of discovery and anticipation of that first touch, that first kiss and that first encounter. Breathe will leave you breathless and craving for more!"
--Lee Hayes, Author of *Passion Marks* **&** *A Deeper Blue*

"Blair R. Poole's debut is a coming-of-age story of discovery and acceptance set against the backdrop of hip-hop and teen urban life. An attention grabber!"
--Frederick Smith, Author of *Down For Whatever*

BREATHE

BY

BLAIR R. POOLE

Burrow Publishing, LLC
Princeton, New Jersey

Cover Design:	Marion Designs www.mariondesigns.com
Book Layout:	Lisa Gibson-Wilson Renaissance Studio of Design www.renmanserv.com
Editor:	Kevin L. Carter

Library of Congress Control Number: 2005907031

ISBN 0-9771812-0-0

First printing October 2005

Printed in the United States of America

ACKNOWLEDGMENTS

First and Foremost, I Thank God for blessing me with the gift of writing and the ability to share my talent with others. I also Thank Him for the greatest gift of all -- Life.

Overwhelming love goes to Kevin, Ma, Naseem, Sunil, Grandma, T.R., Hillary, Sasha, Irene, and my belated great-grandmother Irene (Marna) who have always guided me, shown me unconditional support and love, and who have always encouraged me to follow my heart and my dreams.

Overwhelming love also goes to Blair, Landie, Kai, and Sadik for your constant encouragement, unconditional love and support.

Tremendous love to Manny, Rasheid-Ali, and the rest of my extended family and friends who have also shown me unconditional support and love.

To my professors and teachers, especially those at Lawrenceville, who supported my writing, creativity, and vision. Special thanks to Mr. Greenberg (L'ville).

A special shout-out to the Philadelphia Writers Partnership (PWP family)-- Anna, Kim, Cruze, T.L., Karen, Melanie, Stephanie, and Angela. The creativity, caliber of writing, and continued success of this family is phenomenal.

Additional shout-outs and thanks to Justin Hall and GMAD, Trent, Lee, and Fred for your assistance, advice, and support. I appreciate everything.

A word or two to those who have come and gone out of my life. Each day was a lesson learned and each day brought me closer to the realization of my dream. Each day made me stronger, more confident, and much more mature. If it weren't for some of the experiences (some good, some wonderful, some bad, some traumatic), I may not have been at this point in my life. Thank you.

And, lastly, thanks to all my readers who show love and support. Your words of encouragement keep me motivated and inspired. Thanks for the emails and letters.

About Blair R. Poole

Blair R. Poole is a multi-faceted individual who has worked in the entertainment and legal fields in various capacities for more than seven years. He has been writing for even longer. Since his youth, he always aspired to work in the entertainment business and to become a great screenwriter and novelist. Well, here he is- finally! With his debut novella, *BREATHE*, Blair intends to add his name to the roster of talented authors.

Blair is also a graduate of renowned Drexel University, located in Philadelphia, Pennsylvania, and of the prestigious Lawrenceville School, located in Lawrenceville, New Jersey.

Please visit his website at: **www.blairrpoole.com**

BREATHE

CHAPTER 1

7:17 p.m. on a cold, Sunday evening in mid-January. A fierce winter breeze blew across the streets of Philadelphia. A little more than eight inches of snow packed the ground. The streets were desolate except for the city workers covering the icy ground with rock salt. The waxing, silvery moon shined in the night sky.

Despite the harsh weather, a boisterous birthday party started up on 51st and Spruce Street, disturbing the night's calm. Inside the West Philadelphia residence, dozens of high school teenagers populated the first floor family room and living room, dancing and socializing as Jadakiss' newest joint blasted through the speakers. DJ Q, who was stationed in the living room, spun fiercely in the corner. The powerful bass and hip-hop beats reverberated from the hardwood floor on up, shaking the floor, shaking the walls. Everyone was partying hard, having a good time.

On the left side of the living room, near the picture window, a small, select group of females stood, talking, pointing, and smiling at a handsome caramel-colored brotha, dancing solo. This young man, who was exhibiting his superior dancing skills and outdoing everyone on the dance floor, was Nafiq Johnson- the 17-year-old birthday boy. He was an intelligent brotha, standing 6'3" with a strong athletic build. His powerful physique was a result of his demanding workout regimen, a baseline requirement of his high school basketball team, for which he had been the starting shooting guard for three years. His intelligence was a result of his driven nature, his genes, and his family upbringing. Nafiq sported intricately styled cornrows, an Allen Iverson Sixers jersey, and low-hanging, baggy designer jeans with spotless Timbs. Like many Philly brothas of his generation, he projected a youthful, thuggish masculinity. He was the quintessential hip-hop teenager.

From the kitchen doorway, Gwendolyn and Reginald Johnson stood, observing the party and proudly smiling at their son. Gwendolyn was an attractive, distinguished-looking woman in her mid-50s. Her beautiful auburn hair hung to her shoulders and complimented her soft, honeysuckle skin. As a seasoned paralegal at one of Philly's most prestigious law firms and an active member of the city's largest African Methodist

Episcopal (AME) church, she assumed an air of authority and commanded respect.

Reginald Johnson, a tall, stout, and handsome man also in his mid-50s, was normally a quiet, reserved guy although he did have his moments. He wore a lightly trimmed, graying beard, which created a slight shade against his dark skin, giving him a middle-aged sexiness. As a young man, he was a star tight end at Cheyney University and, later, an officer in the Navy SEALs. Now, he was the sole proprietor of Kool Kutz barbershop in Southwest Philly- going strong for nearly 20 years. Reginald was also active in the community. He routinely volunteered at the city's homeless shelters, and coached recreational football for 5th and 6th graders.

Together, Reginald and Gwendolyn projected a uniquely Black yin-yang as they affectionately held each other, and cheered Nafiq on.

After showing off his skills on the dance floor, Nafiq rolled up to Simone, a pretty, voluptuous young woman who was one of Nafiq's classmates at Central High School. Like Nafiq, she was among the most attractive and sought after individuals there. She was a star sprinter on the track team, and her grades placed her in the top five of her class. Simone danced close to Nafiq, enjoying herself immensely. He appeared to be enjoying himself as well. Throughout the room, envious eyes lingered on the two as they danced. However, Nafiq and Simone ignored their peers' jealously and continued to dance until DJ Q mixed into another song.

"I'll be back in a sec," Nafiq said.

"Where are you going? We just started dancing," huffed Simone.

"Just chill. I'll be right back."

Nafiq escaped the crowd, and walked into the hallway, leaving Simone in the middle of the dance floor. She folded her arms tightly, disappointed.

In the hallway, Nafiq took a seat on the hardwood stairs, and wiped sweat from his forehead. He sat placidly, looking out into the crowd; his expression inscrutable. As he looked into the crowd, his sister, Kiara, an alluringly beautiful and high-spirited woman, strolled up to him. Only twenty-six years old, this almond-colored sista was a diamond; a down-to-earth sweetheart with talent and intelligence. After graduating summa cum laude with a degree in fashion design from the Rhode Island School of Design, she decided to take the entrepreneurial route, like her father, and open up her own clothing boutique in the city.

"Fiq, why are you sitting down? You're supposed to be celebrating," Kiara said, excited.

She grabbed Nafiq's hand, but he resisted. His face remained placid, his feelings a mystery.

"Sis, I'll be there," he said.

Nafiq's resistance stunned Kiara. She looked at him closely, trying to figure out what was on her brother's mind.

"Are you all right? Did something happen out there?"

"Naw, I'm cool."

Kiara exhibited some skepticism. She knew her little brother, and she knew that something was wrong. Since they were children, she could always sense when something troubled him, especially when others failed to detect a problem.

"Are you sure you're all right?" she asked, her eyebrow arching.

"Kiara, I'm fine. I'll be there. Aight?" Nafiq said in a mildly irritated tone.

"Okay," Kiara said as she shrugged her shoulders and walked away. But before she completely entered the living room, she stopped, turned around, and looked at Nafiq. He seemed deeply troubled, and was reluctant to share what was on his mind. Over the past few months, Kiara felt that Nafiq had been acting distant. She constantly asked him if something were bothering him, but he continuously ensured her that nothing was wrong. "Nothing!"

Kiara frowned to herself, and decided to leave her brother alone. She didn't want to anger or annoy Nafiq by pressing him, especially on his birthday. She turned back around, and returned to the living room.

Meanwhile, Nafiq stayed on the steps, and stared into the living room. He watched his male and female peers dance and flirt with each other. He saw one couple kiss. Another couple held hands in the corner as they bopped happily to the music. This bothered Nafiq deeply. He longed for the same affection, for the same feelings of elation, joy and comfort. He yearned for that special connection with someone. He longed to truly express himself.

A look of deep sadness quickly grew over Nafiq's face.

He couldn't stomach these displays of affection and happiness anymore, so he rose from the stairs, quickly concealed his emotions, and walked into the living room.

As Nafiq entered the living room, Gwendolyn took his arm and escorted him to the glass, dining table where his elaborate birthday cake sat.

"It's time to sing 'Happy Birthday,'" his mother informed, smiling.

Nafiq stood at the table. Everyone gathered around the fragrant, sugar-laden cake, and broke into a soulful rendition of "Happy Birthday." Kiara finished the song with some sultry ad-libs.

Nafiq leaned over the cake, and tightly closed his eyes. The intense glow of the candles illuminated his face. He silently made a wish and opened up his eyes. He blew out the candles all at once, and everyone clapped. A few people whistled and cheered. His closest friends and a few flirtatious girls wished him a "Happy Birthday," and patted him on the back. He graciously nodded and thanked them.

The crowd moved in closer as Gwendolyn handed Nafiq the knife to slice the cake. He started passing the cake around, and everyone began to eat.

Nafiq picked up his plastic plate, and took a bite of his cake. The cake was one of his mom's typical gourmet choices- chocolate with a praline, buttercream icing. It was hypnotizingly sweet. But Nafiq was neither impressed nor satisfied. To him, it was just another cake. Another party and birthday. Just another damn day.

The Johnson family stood next to him, eating and enjoying the cake.

"Happy Birthday," Gwendolyn and Reginald said almost simultaneously.

"Thanks, Mom. Dad," Nafiq responded.

Nafiq's only brother, Marcus Johnson, patted Nafiq on the back. The 21-year-old college senior wore a University of Pennsylvania Wharton School sweater with sandy-brown khakis. Marcus wasn't as tall as Nafiq (he was only 5'10"), but he was just as *phine*. His hazelnut skin, medium build, and dark eyelashes, which emphasized his light brown eyes, drove women wild.

"Happy Birthday, man," Marcus said.

"Thanks."

Alonzo Miller, Kiara's boyfriend of four years, wished him "Happy Birthday" and handed him three, crisp $100 bills. Surprised, Nafiq showed one of his few real smiles of the night and stuffed the cash into his pocket.

"Thanks, Zo," said Nafiq.

Alonzo smiled and nodded.

Alonzo, on the cusp of thirty years old, was a vain and pretentious individual. He always dressed to perfection in designer clothes- Armani attire being his preference- and was always meticulously groomed. He was distinguished by his nicely styled dreadlocks, which fell to the middle of his back. He also routinely bragged about his surplus of cash and his high-paying A&R job at Philly's most reputable record company, Triple-P Records, Inc. A Morehouse grad and a

M.B.A. recipient from Temple University's business program, Alonzo knew he was destined for greatness.

Kiara, who stood with Alonzo's arm around her waist, broke away from him and gave Nafiq a big hug.

"Happy Birthday. I love you," said Kiara.

"Thanks. Love you, too," responded Nafiq as he kissed his sister on the cheek.

Alonzo interrupted the family love by tapping Nafiq on the shoulder and nodding his head in the direction of someone across the room. Nafiq turned his head, and noticed Simone standing by herself. Other guys were clearly staring at her, debating whether or not to approach her, but her eyes were fastened on Nafiq.

"Man, you better go get yours," Marcus insisted.

But before Nafiq could step away, Simone walked up to him, smiling. She reached out her right hand.

"It's time for that birthday dance. I made a special request," she said.

The Johnson family, especially Gwendolyn, looked impressed by Simone's confidence and forwardness. She saw a bit of herself in the assertive teen. After all, not just any female was good enough for her son. In fact, Gwendolyn and Reginald had worked too hard and struggled too long for any of their children to just date anybody, to just marry anybody, or to just socialize with anybody. Reginald and Gwendolyn grew up poor and resided in a lower middle-class African-American community, but they believed that their purpose was to help uplift their community. To be pillars and mentors. To share some of their success with others. To be an inspiration for others. They truly believed that each generation is supposed to improve. With "Elevate" as their mantra, they were determined to help others, especially their children, take it to the next level.

Nafiq smiled, and took Simone's hand. They walked to the middle of the dance floor. DJ Q expertly moved from an up-tempo song into a slow jam. The lights dimmed, creating a sensual, romantic mood. As Nafiq and Simone began to dance, the crowd slowly closed in, enveloping them.

✠

In Nafiq's bedroom, posters of hip-hop artists and NBA ballers shared space with gorgeous swimsuit models from magazines such as *King* and *Black Men*. His bookshelves were covered with numerous academic achievement awards, trophies, plaques, snapshots of himself with family and friends, and pictures of him proudly posing with Central's basketball team.

Nafiq, dressed in navy blue boxers and a white wifebeater, sat at his desk in front of the computer monitor. It was a quarter after midnight, and his party had been over for a little over an hour. He surfed the Internet- his concentration very intense.

On the computer monitor, the cursor found and selected a link: www.4myniggaz.com. A small window popped up, and a nude white female with flowing blonde hair began to caress herself seductively. Her hands squeezed her large, supple breasts. She moaned in ecstasy as she stared at Nafiq with her crystalline blue eyes- eyes that were meant to captivate and entice.

Nafiq watched with indifference. He clicked the mouse, closing the pop-up. He turned the volume down on his computer's speakers and then clicked the cursor on the [ENTER] link. Soon thereafter, color images of all types of nude African-American and Latino men slowly loaded onto the screen. Muscular, washboard stomach bois from the South. Tattoo-laden, Los Angeles thugs with shaved heads and goatees. Butterscotch and mocha-skinned, stocky brothas from NYC. The selection was plentiful.

Nafiq grinned as he stared with lustful eyes. His temperature climbed. His manhood enlarged.

The computer cursor jogged across the screen, hunting for the right image. That image that would make him nut.

Nafiq clicked the mouse and an image enlarged, displaying a naked, nutmeg-colored African-American male- thuggish, tattooed, and athletic. The image began to gesticulate, and chant "You want some of dis, nigga?"

Nafiq stared at the image, growing deeply entranced. He touched the screen with his index finger, slowly outlining the contours of the image's physique. The image smoothed his hand over his own chiseled chest, and slid it down past his belly button, leading to his bulging crotch. Nafiq slipped his right hand underneath his boxers, and started to stroke himself. He inhaled and exhaled deeply, each breath becoming more and more intense until- KNOCK! KNOCK! There was someone at the door!

Nafiq swiftly jumped up, knocking the mouse to the floor. He frantically picked it up, clicked an icon to minimize the image, and clicked another icon, which displayed a history paper.

"Come in," Nafiq stammered.

Reginald entered the room, and stumbled across the mess on the floor, almost tripping. Reginald sat on the edge of Nafiq's bed.

"Boy, I almost killed myself. Didn't I tell you to clean up this room a couple days ago?"

"I'm sorry, Dad. I'll clean up tomorrow. I've just been preoccupied with school."

He glanced over at the computer screen.

"Doing schoolwork this late?" Reginald asked, surprised.

He knew that Nafiq finished his assignments early, and never worked past eleven o'clock at night.

"Oh… I just wanted to make a few edits while it was still on my mind," Nafiq responded.

Reginald studied Nafiq briefly, skeptical.

Nafiq sat at his desk, hands innocently clasped together, with a nervous look on his face. His piece was still aroused, and tucked tightly (very tightly) between his thighs. One slight move and he would be exposed.

"Is everything okay?" Reginald asked.

"Yeah, Dad. Everything's cool."

Reginald nodded, and changed the subject. "How'd you

like your party?"

"For a Sunday party during a blizzard, the turn out was great. I had the time of my life."

"I bet you did. That girl, Simone, really likes you."

Nafiq smiled. "I know."

"From what I see, she'd be a nice choice for you. She's smart. And I hear she plans to become a pediatrician someday. And you already know she's a sexy young lady."

"True," Nafiq responded.

"So... are you thinking about dating her? Tell your old man."

"Well, I don't mind chillin' with her, but I don't want to commit myself to any type of relationship right now. I just want to enjoy myself."

Reginald smiled. "I understand. You want to play the field. I remember when I was your age. The ladies were all over me. They couldn't get enough of Reggie Run-em-over Johnson. But I did have to be careful, because they saw promise and a good future, and that's when some females try to get you. But I'm glad you're trying to be smart and careful, too."

"No doubt," responded Nafiq.

"You're using protection?" Reginald bluntly asked.

"Yeah, Dad. Of course."

"Just checking. I don't want any grandkids from you anytime soon. I also want you to be a healthy man."

"I understand," said Nafiq.

Reginald rose from the bed, and patted Nafiq on his back.

"Well, I just wanted to check up on you before I went to bed. I'll see you in the morning."

"All right, Dad. Have a good night."

"You, too," Reginald said before exiting the room, and closing the door behind himself.

Nafiq waited about a minute, listening carefully for his parents' bedroom door to close. Once he heard the door shut, he turned toward the computer screen with anticipation. He pulled his boxers down to his ankles, and clicked an icon on the computer. The naked male popped back onto the screen. He clicked off the image, and started to scan other pictures of sexy, African-American and Latino men.

CHAPTER 2

Shawn, Nafiq's best friend since kindergarten, sat on the sofa, and stared blankly at the hardwood floor, waiting for Nafiq to finish getting dressed. Shawn stood 6 feet tall, had a medium build, and was very handsome. He sported designer urban gear and a large, unkempt fro with a pick in it. Ya know, one of them old-style '70s picks with the black power fist at the end. His empty book bag lay next to him. His hand propped his head up as he waited impatiently for Nafiq.

"Yo, Fiq. Hurry up," yelled Shawn. "It's almost a quarter after 8. I don't need another detention."

A few minutes later, Nafiq walked down the stairs, and entered the living room sluggishly and sleepily. He was exhausted from his nightlong activities of surfing for X-rated pictures online and instant messaging fellas from the www.4myniggaz.com chat group.

He walked over to Shawn, and gave him their signature handshake. "Wassup?"

"Wassup? You ready?" asked Shawn.

"Yeah. Come on."

Shawn rose from the sofa, and walked with Nafiq toward the front door. They left the house, and began walking down the street. Snow fell from the gray, overcast sky. There were teenagers in front of them and behind them, all walking in the same direction. In the distance, Central High School could be seen.

"Yo, Fiq, your party was the shit. I haven't got down like that in a long time. And check this out."

Shawn took out a wrinkled piece of paper from his coat pocket, and handed it to Nafiq.

"What's this?" Nafiq asked.

"Cherice's number."

Nafiq gave Shawn a pound. "It's 'bout time. You been chasin' her for months."

"Man, whatever," replied Shawn.

Nafiq laughed.

"So you and Simone together yet?" Shawn asked curiously. "Ya'll definitely seemed together at your party."

"Naw, we ain't together. I'm feelin' her, but I want to explore all my options."

"Are you gonna tap it, at least? I bet that shit is aight."

"I want to, but I think she wants us to be exclusive, and I ain't with that."

"I guess you not taking her to Tamika's Valentine's Day party, then?"

"Naw."

"Good. 'Cause you know it's gonna be off da fuckin' hook. All kinds of freaks are gonna be there. Shit. I'm gonna get my jawn wet all night long."

"I feel that," Nafiq nodded in agreement.

"So what's the plan for later on?" Shawn asked.

"I got practice, a test to study for, and I gotta stop by my Dad's shop."

"In other words, you not chillin' wit me?"

"I can't."

"Man, I just got the latest Grand Theft Auto, and Cherice invited us to chill wit her and her peoples. You really tellin' me you don't wanna hang?"

"Hell yeah, I wanna hang, but I got stuff to do."

"Like I told you before, all you do is study and practice. You need to chill a lil' bit, especially now. This is your birthday. You're supposed to celebrate for two weeks straight."

"I feel you, but I gotta be on point. My grades and my ball playin' are priority right now. You know I wanna go to Duke."

Shawn looked away, exhibiting some jealously. With Shawn's D average, matriculation at a private college or university was certainly out of the question. He wanted to attend college. In fact, he would be the first person in his family to do so. However, his mother's lack of expectations for him, and her frequent taunts of how he was a "no-good nigga" and "wouldn't amount to shit" like his absentee father badly impacted his self-esteem and contributed to his outwardly uncaring, unmotivated persona.

"It's all good. When a busy brotha has some time, make sure he calls his boi. Aight?"

"A busy brotha will definitely do that."

Nafiq and Shawn entered the front gates of the high school. They passed a group of male students, huddled in a close circle, smoking weed, and greeted them by nodding their heads. Nafiq and Shawn walked up the concrete steps, leading to large, double doors, and entered the school.

Nafiq and Shawn walked down the long, yellow-walled corridor, forcing their way through the large group of students. They turned down another long hallway, and went to their lockers, which were next to each other. Shawn took some CDs and his disc player out of his locker, and stuffed them into his book bag. Nafiq took a few books from his locker, and put them into his book bag. They closed their lockers.

"Aight. I'll see you at lunch," said Shawn.

They gave each other a pound.

"Aight, peace," Nafiq replied.

Shawn walked down one extension of the hallway while Nafiq walked down the other toward his first period class.

As Nafiq entered the classroom, the bell rang. He took a seat at a desk, and took out his Calculus textbook and notebook. Mrs. Jackson, a bookish African-American teacher in her mid-thirties, stood in front of the classroom, drawing graphs and writing equations on the blackboard. The top of the blackboard read: AP Calculus.

Lamar was the last person to enter the classroom. Standing 5'11" with a smooth, cocoa complexion, he projected a vaguely feminine vibe. He didn't partake in the switching, finger snapping, or smacking of the lips, but it was clear that he was ...well... you know. Lamar closed the door, and took a seat at a desk diagonally behind Nafiq. There were only eleven students in the classroom. Mrs. Jackson turned to face the front of the class.

"Good morning, class," she said, pleasantly.

The class greeted Mrs. Jackson.

Mrs. Jackson continued, "If everyone would turn to pg. 257. I'm going to discuss the section on indefinite integrals before we go over yesterday's quiz."

The class turned to the requested page, and Mrs. Jackson began to lecture.

Nafiq sat at his desk in a sleepy daze. For ten minutes, he tried to prevent himself from dozing off, but this feat proved too difficult. His eyes blinked open and shut. Mrs. Jackson's words faded in and out and gradually became inaudible. He desperately fought to stay awake, but to no avail. He quickly drifted into a reverie...

Nafiq, dressed only in workout shorts, was lifting weights in the school gym. Suddenly, a nude African-American male entered the gym, and strutted toward Nafiq. It was the same chiseled, tattoo-laden thug from the www.4myniggaz.com site. Beads of sweat glistened on his muscular body. The thug looked at the weight bench, and then looked at Nafiq with a devilish grin.

"How 'bout I spot you?" the thug asked.

Nafiq held the weights, frozen in place. The thug moved closer to Nafiq, sliding his hand across his chest, and seductively biting his full lips. Nafiq started to back away.

"Naw… I don't get down like that man. Chill wit dat. Aight?" Nafiq said.

The thug forcefully grabbed the weights from Nafiq, and threw them to the floor. He then pinched Nafiq's nipple and grabbed his crotch. Nafiq was aroused.

"How 'bout I take care of dis fo' ya?" the thug asked as he tightened his grip.

Nafiq nodded.

They slowly sought out each other's lips, and before they kissed--

SWACK! Mrs. Jackson slapped her yardstick against the metal desk. Nafiq, startled, quickly lifted his head. He looked around the classroom at all the students watching him, and shifted self-consciously. His eyes locked with Lamar's, and Lamar raised his eyebrows. Mrs. Jackson loudly called out Nafiq's name. He whipped his head around, and looked at Mrs. Jackson.

"Are you okay, Mr. Johnson? It sounded as if you were

really enjoying that nap," Mrs. Jackson teased.

The class broke out into laughter.

Nafiq was frozen in place. Embarrassed. Humiliated. He had only hoped that he didn't utter any verbal references to the thug in his daydream.

"All right, class. Settle down," Mrs. Jackson told her students.

She faced Nafiq, again. "I was telling the class that you were the only student to get the bonus question correct on the quiz, and I wanted you to come up here and show everyone how to do it."

Mrs. Jackson extended her arm out, with chalk in hand, and motioned for Nafiq to come to the blackboard. Nafiq lowered his arms, covering his crotch. His stiffness was not letting up. He hesitated, and then squirmed, trying to reposition *it*.

"Nafiq, come up here now. The class ends in a few minutes," said Mrs. Jackson, growing increasingly agitated.

Nafiq began to slowly inch off his seat, but before he could stand up, the bell rang.

The students quickly gathered their books and belongings to leave the classroom. Nafiq, slouched in his seat, took a long, deep sigh of relief. Mrs. Jackson stood at her desk, shaking her head in dismay.

✠

The food line at the crowded school cafeteria was long as students jostled and socialized with each other, waiting to pay for and receive their food. The smell of greasy french fries, hot dogs, and hamburgers filled the air. Lunch aides, all dour-faced black women in their 50s and 60s, served the boisterous crowd of students.

Shawn and Jayson sat at the long table, observing a group of girls who had just strolled into the lunchroom. Jayson was a thin, light-skinned, freckle-faced Jamaican brotha who had emigrated to Philly with his family when he was seven years old. He'd been in the United States for a decade, but he still spoke with a strong Jamaican accent. He sported a red, green, and gold Bob Marley shirt.

"Dayum! She's fine as Hell," said Jayson.

"Yes, she is. Damn!" Shawn agreed.

Shawn's and Jayson's lustful eyes followed the girls as they took a seat at a table far across the cafeteria. The girls noticed Jayson and Shawn watching. They smiled flirtatiously at Shawn, but sneered at Jayson. Jayson frowned.

Nafiq walked up to the table with his tray of food, and took a seat.

"What's good, ya'll?" asked Nafiq.

"Check out them cuties over there!" instructed Shawn.

Shawn nodded his head in the direction of the girls, who were no longer looking at Shawn and Jayson. They were too busy conversing among themselves.

Nafiq took a sip of his soda.

"Where'd they come from? They look good," said Nafiq.

"I think they freshmen," said Shawn.

"But you probably not interested anyway since you kickin' it wit-"

Jayson's silent motion indicated that the person had big breasts and a thick, shapely ass.

"Man, you late as usual. Fiq, ain't feelin' Simone like that," said Shawn.

"What? Then, who was you fantasizing about in Jackson's class?" asked Jayson, perplexed.

Nafiq's eyes bulged.

Shawn nudged Jayson's arm.

"What?" asked Nafiq, tense.

"I heard you were having some off da hook dream in your Calc class," said Jayson.

Shawn cut a thin smile.

Nafiq looked stunned.

"Where'd you hear that?" Nafiq asked, concerned.

"Everybody in my 5th period," responded Jayson.

"Actually, a lot of people heard about it. It was probably Danielle from your class. You know she got a big mouth," said Shawn.

"I wasn't dreaming about anyone," Nafiq said, defensively.

"Come on, Fiq. We bois. You can tell us," urged Shawn.

Nafiq slammed his drink down, splattering soda onto the table.

"Yo! I told ya'll I wasn't having a dream. Just drop it. Damn!" said Nafiq.

"Aight, playa. Calm down," said Shawn.

"Yeah. Didn't mean to make a brotha hostile," said Jayson.

Nafiq, bothered, sat at the table, silently, picking at his food.

✠

Inside the high school, Lamar and Julian walked down the hallway. Julian was what most people considered a "pretty boy." He was light-skinned and had mesmerizing gray eyes, silky smooth skin, and soft wavy hair. He was, like Lamar, somewhat effeminate, but not blatantly so. Lamar and Julian had been friends since seventh grade.

Lamar stopped, and peeked into the gymnasium window. The basketball team was practicing. Some players were shooting. Others ran up and down the length of the court, practicing their crossover dribbles. Nafiq, number 11, stood behind the arc, launching three-pointers. His shooting was effortless.

"Look. You see number 11?" asked Lamar.

Julian looked through the gym window. "Yeah."

"That's who I was telling you about," Lamar said. He chuckled to himself. "I still can't believe he was having some triple X dream up in class. Moanin' and groanin' and carryin' on."

Julian laughed, and looked through the window, again. He paused for a short moment, contemplating something. Then:

"He doesn't look like he messes around."

"Boy, you should have seen the look he gave me in class."

"Please, Mar. To hear you tell it, everyone gives you that look," said Julian, incredulously.

"I'm serious."

"Well, if he is on the DL, you better be careful. You know how those DL boys are," Julian warned.

Lamar turned away from Julian, and looked back through the gym window, anxiously. He watched Nafiq practice his shots.

"I'll be fine," said Lamar, assuredly.

Julian tugged on Lamar's arm. "Stop salivating, and come on. He's not going anywhere. But the sale at Banana Republic is."

Lamar turned away from the window, and nodded his head in agreement. They rushed down the hallway toward the school's exit.

✠

Kool Kutz barbershop was crowded with patrons of all ages. Afrocentric art hung on the walls, as well as pictures of Reginald posing in the shop with various celebrities who had gotten a cut at the shop.

There were four chairs, a barber manning each. All were working on clients' heads. Reginald had the first chair- the chair of honor. He sported a gold-colored, custom-made barber's cape with "Reggie" embroidered on the front.

Patrons, including Marcus and Alonzo, watched and fervently discussed a Comcast On-Demand rebroadcast of a recent Sixers game.

Nafiq entered the shop, carrying his gym bag on his shoulder. He greeted everyone with a nod or comment as he walked toward Reginald. Mr. Fulton, one of Reginald's longtime clients, sat in a chair, getting his hair cut by Reginald.

"What's up, Dad?"

"Hi, son," Reginald responded.

Nafiq firmly shook Mr. Fulton's hand, and greeted him.

"How are you, Mr. Fulton?"

"Couldn't be better," replied Mr. Fulton, in his 55-year-old bass voice. "How about yourself?"

"I'm good," replied Nafiq.

"I hear your championship is in a few weeks," said Mr. Fulton.

"Yeah. Make sure you come out and support," Nafiq insisted.

"Oh, I intend to."

Reginald reached into his pocket, and pulled out some birthday cash for Nafiq. He handed it to him. Nafiq smiled, and thanked his father.

Marcus and Alonzo got up from their seats, and walked over to Nafiq.

"It's about time you got here. We've been waiting for you," said Marcus.

"Why?" asked Nafiq.

"I just got a new ride, and I wanted to take you and Marcus for a spin," informed Alonzo.

"That's what's up. Let's roll out," said Nafiq.

Nafiq, Marcus, and Alonzo said goodbye to Reginald, and headed out the shop.

Outside, Alonzo walked up to his shining, brand-new, midnight-black Mercedes-Benz. Nafiq and Marcus followed him to the car, and examined it in awe. Alonzo proudly watched them.

"This is nice and about $80,000. Where did you get the funds for this?" asked Marcus, curiously.

"It was a gift from my company," responded Alonzo, nonchalantly.

"True? Can I be you?" said Nafiq.

"What was the gift for?" inquired Marcus, still checking out the car.

"A few weeks back, I spotted this hot female, hip-hop group performing in one of the underground clubs. I took them to see the president of my label. They did their thing for him, and it was history from there. We're grooming them to be the next TLC," said Alonzo.

"That's what's up. Congratulations," said Nafiq.

Alonzo took out his keys, and pressed a remote control pad. The car doors clicked open.

"Let's go," Alonzo instructed.

They got into the car. Nafiq sat in the back while Marcus rode shotgun. Alonzo started the engine and pulled off. He drove toward Center City Philadelphia. The city's premier R&B/hip hop radio station played in the background as the three men talked about the Eagles, women, the Sixers, women, politics, women, and more women. And, of course, Alonzo, feelin' it, bragged about his high-paying A&R job, how he was better and more educated than everyone, and how he would someday rule his own music empire. Suddenly, in the middle of his talk, Alonzo abruptly stopped the car.

Police barricades blocked two of the city streets, greatly slowing the flow of traffic. A police officer redirected traffic onto 13th street- the city's infamous, gay strip. Nafiq looked out the car window, watching the colorful, rainbow flags on the lampposts gracefully undulate, as they approached 13th street. Alonzo grimaced, and turned onto the street, driving northbound towards Market Street. A stoplight turned red, and Alonzo stopped the car. Men of color of all ages hung out on the corner despite the wintry weather.

Nafiq, Alonzo, and Marcus looked out the car window at the bustling scene. Nafiq scanned the area with an intrigued eye. There were trendy nightclubs and coffee bars all around. The bright, neon signs of the X-rated theaters shined spectacularly. Just about all of the passersby appeared happy and in good spirits. Two black males, holding hands, walked into a club.

Marcus shook his head in disgust. "Look at that. Disgusting."

"Faggots make me sick to my stomach," growled Alonzo.

Nafiq quickly concealed any signs of intrigue or interest.

Alonzo turned his head, and saw Lamar walking toward the car with a group of teenagers. Lamar curiously peered inside the car, and cast a furtive glance to Alonzo. Alonzo turned his head. Nafiq's and Lamar's eyes met. Lamar smirked, and continued to walk past the car with his friends. The stoplight turned green, and Alonzo quickly sped off, heading back to the Johnson residence.

"They need to keep that shit to themselves. Those homos do nothing but degrade Black men's manhood. It's hard enough as it is," said Alonzo.

Marcus shook his head, appalled.

Nafiq chided in. "Yeah. That's some nasty shit."

CHAPTER 3

Blustery winds blew, causing the branches of bare trees to make high-pitched whipping sounds. Snow and sharp icicles fell from roofs of houses and power lines.

In the evening darkness, Lamar walked down the street toward his home. In the short distance, he spotted a figure in a familiar black and gray winter coat crossing the street. It was Nafiq. He had just finished basketball practice, and was on his way home, too. Lamar smiled to himself, and rushed up to Nafiq.

"Yo, what's up?" asked Lamar.

Nafiq turned around, and stopped. He responded coldly.

"Do I know you?"

Lamar rebuffed Nafiq's coldness.

"I'm in your Calc class. I sit in the back."

"Oh," said Nafiq, seemingly uncaring.

An awkward silence prevailed for a few moments. Nafiq picked up his walking pace, nervously looking around. He knew who Lamar was, and didn't want to be seen in public with him. Nafiq had heard rumors from fellow classmates that Lamar was gay, and, based on subtle mannerisms in class, his stroll down 13th street, and this brief exchange, Nafiq believed the rumors to be true.

"Weren't you downtown the other night?" asked Lamar.

"Why you wanna know?" asked Nafiq with an intimidating stare.

Lamar wasn't fazed by Nafiq's stare. He understood the game. He knew that the look was just a front.

"I thought I may have seen you cruising the area?" Lamar said, smirking. He gave Nafiq a knowing nod.

Nafiq felt invaded now, and upset that he had been read by Lamar.

"Look, man. What do you want?" Nafiq said with indignation.

"I was just trying to see what was good."

"Nothing's good. And I don't like being interrogated. Aight?"

"I apologize. You seemed cool, and I was just trying to make conversation," said Lamar.

Another moment of awkward silence prevailed. Lamar appeared to be trying to think of something to say. Then:

"Did you study for the quiz yet?"

"A little," replied Nafiq, slightly hesitant.

"I haven't yet. I'll probably start after the Sixers game tonight."

"You watch ball?" asked Nafiq, surprised.

"Absolutely. The Sixers is my team," exclaimed Lamar, lying through his teeth.

"Mine, too."

"Cool. Why don't you come watch the game over my house tonight? Afterwards, we can have a study session."

Nafiq looked at Lamar briefly, and turned away. He pondered the invitation. Nafiq was curious to see what Lamar was all about, but going to Lamar's house would be risky. Real risky. He decided to decline.

"Can't."

"It'll be all right. Come on," Lamar persisted.

Lamar gave Nafiq a pressuring look.

Nafiq hesitated for a moment, contemplating a little further.

"Sorry. I already got plans."

"Okay," said Lamar.

"I'll get at you later," said Nafiq before rushing across the street and continuing his walk home.

Lamar stopped, and stood on the sidewalk, disappointed at his failed attempt.

However, this wasn't the end of the road. Lamar was determined to get Nafiq. To entice him. To sample him.

CHAPTER 4

Friday afternoon. Right after third period. Nafiq leaned against his locker, telling jokes and stories to Kim and Janet, two of his classmates.

"Nafiq, you're so funny," Kim chuckled as she rubbed and squeezed his arm.

"Intelligent, athletic, and a great sense of humor. Simone's a lucky sista," Janet added.

"Nafiq isn't dating Simone," asserted Kim. She curiously looked at Nafiq for official confirmation.

"We *ain't* dating," said Nafiq.

Kim smiled, and grabbed onto Nafiq's arm, again, squeezing tighter.

"Well, I want you come over my house tomorrow. I'm throwing a party, and it's mandatory that you come."

"And make sure you bring your boi, Shawn, too," said Janet.

"We'll be there."

Kim sensuously pinched Nafiq's chin. "Great. I'll see you tomorrow."

"Bye," said Janet.

"Peace," Nafiq told Kim and Janet as they started to walk away.

Nafiq turned around, and started taking books from his locker.

Lamar walked down the hallway toward Nafiq, and stopped at his locker.

Shawn and Jayson, who were also walking down the hallway, noticed Lamar standing next to Nafiq, conversing. They stopped, and observed from afar.

"What's up?" greeted Lamar.

Nafiq frowned at Lamar, and looked around nervously. He quickly took his books out of his locker, and shoved them into his book bag.

"Yo, what are you doin'?" asked Nafiq, paranoid.

"There's another Sixers game tonight. I wanted to invite you to my house, again," Lamar said.

"Maybe another time. I'm chillin' with my peoples tonight," Nafiq said, closing his locker.

Lamar handed him a piece of paper. "Here's my address, cell number, and IM if you change your mind."

Nafiq took the paper, and quickly shoved it into his jeans pocket without looking at it.

Nafiq turned, and saw Jayson and Shawn, watching he and Lamar talk. He immediately rushed toward Shawn and Jayson without saying anything further to Lamar.

Lamar stood at the locker, insulted and hurt.

"Yo, wassup?" Nafiq asked Shawn and Jayson.

They looked at him bewildered.

"Why you talkin' to dude?" asked Shawn.

"Who?"

"Boy at your locker," Shawn indicated.

"We're in the same Calc class. He had a few questions. Why?"

"He's gay."

"For real?" questioned Nafiq, trying to play off the situation.

"That's what people say. So you betta watch your back. He might try to pull somethin'. Then, we'd have to go kick his batty boy ass," said Jayson.

"No need. I can handle myself. I don't get down like that anyway. I love my sexy, black sistas," said Nafiq.

"True," responded Shawn and Jayson.

Shawn, Jayson, and Nafiq gave each other pounds.

✠

Simone and Tracey sat in the bleachers of the high school gymnasium, watching basketball practice. Tracey was one of Simone's closest friends. She had a milk chocolate complexion and wore a close-cropped hairstyle with tints of lavender and beige. She was pretty and also outspoken. Tracey elbowed Simone to get up.

"Girl, I wish you'd stop procrastinating. We don't have all day. If you like the boy, then ask him to the party," insisted Tracey.

"I don't want to seem desperate or pushy," said Simone.

"You won't. Now go!"

Simone hesitated for a moment, and took a deep breath. She stood up, and walked down the steps toward the basketball court. She skirted along the wooden bleachers, and then stopped at the sideline. She called Nafiq's name. Nafiq was concentrating on his game, and didn't hear Simone. She called his name, again.

Brian, one of Nafiq's teammates, heard Simone, and tapped Nafiq on the shoulder. "Nafiq, some lil' cutie is tryin' to get at you."

Nafiq looked over to the sideline, and saw Simone. He jogged over to her.

"Hey, wassup?"

"Hi. I just wanted to see how you were doin'? We haven't talked since your party."

"Sorry about that. I've just been real busy."

Nafiq quickly glanced at the other side of the gym where Coach Franklin, a graying 50-something white man, was engaged in conversation with another player.

"But, listen, I really can't talk right now," said Nafiq.

"I know you're busy. I was just wondering if you wanted to go to Tamika's Valentine's party with me?"

Suddenly, a whistle blew. Nafiq turned to look at his coach.

"Nafiq, this isn't social hour!" yelled Coach Franklin.

Nafiq faced Simone, again.

"Yeah, that's cool," Nafiq quickly said.

"Great. Call me later."

"Aight."

Nafiq hustled back onto the court.

Simone excitedly hurried up the steps toward Tracey.

"'Yes?'" asked Tracey.

Simone nodded her head affirmatively.

"Go, girl," said Tracey, giving Simone a high-five.

On the court, Nafiq grabbed a ball and shot it toward the basket. He missed.

✠

Shawn and Jayson waited inside LEE's corner store for the three chicken wings and fried rice they had just ordered. A drunk, overweight female, dressed in a white nightgown and wearing pink house slippers, cursed at Ms. Lee for overcharging her for some cigarettes and condoms. Shawn,

Jayson, and the other store patrons laughed to themselves. After the overweight female left, Shawn's face suddenly turned serious. He tapped Jayson on the arm.

"Yo. You think Nafiq's been acting different lately?"

"A little."

"I think so, too."

"Maybe he think he betta than us now. You know his family's uppity," responded Jayson.

"Naw, it's not that." Shawn frowned up his mouth. "I don't like the fact he was talking to that homo at his locker. The Nafiq I know would of busted dude in the jaw if he even spoke a word to him."

"So what you saying? Nafiq's a batty boy?" asked Jayson.

Shawn stopped and pondered. "Naw. I'm not saying that. He's just getting soft."

Ms. Lee's shrill voice interrupted. "Your order's ready."

They walked up to the Plexiglas window.

"Yo, you wanna smoke," Jayson asked Shawn.

"Yeah."

"Let me get a vanilla dutch, too," Jayson told Ms. Lee as he slipped the money through the side of the window.

Ms. Lee pushed the bag of food and the dutch through the small opening in the window.

They grabbed their stuff, and sat down on a bench inside the store. Jayson took out a bag of weed, and started rolling.

Two brown skinned cuties walked into the store. They smiled at Shawn.

"Ya'll wanna smoke?" Shawn offered.

"Yeah," one of the girls replied.

Shawn turned to Jayson. "See what Nafiq is missing?"

Jayson nodded his head in agreement as he continued to roll.

✠

Nafiq was finally done with basketball practice and on his way home. It was Friday night, and he was bored. He could have chilled with Shawn and Jayson, but he had the urge to change things up a little bit this Friday. After some deep contemplation, he took out a piece of paper, looked at it, and started to dial a number on his cellphone.

"Hello?" a male voice answered.

"Is this Lamar?" Nafiq asked.

"Yeah. Who's this?"

"Nafiq."

Lamar, who was sitting on his sofa talking with Julian, grabbed Julian's arm excitedly. Lamar's face lit up.

"Hey. What's good?" asked Lamar.

"You still watching the game tonight?"

"Yeah. You wanna stop by."

"Yeah. I should be there around 8," informed Nafiq.

"Cool," responded Lamar. "I'll see you when you get here."

"Is there anyone else there?" asked Nafiq.

"No, it's just me. My mom is over my aunt's house, and she won't be back until tomorrow," replied Lamar.

"Aight. I'll see you in a few."

Nafiq hung up his cellphone. He stopped walking, and swallowed hard, not knowing what to expect. He couldn't believe he decided to visit Lamar. He reconsidered his decision, but opted to stick it out.

Meanwhile, at Lamar's house, Lamar turned to Julian.

"Guess who's coming?"

"Carlos?"

"Better. Much, much better."

"Who?"

"Nafiq."

"Stop playing," Julian said, surprised.

"I swear. He'll be here at 8."

"He came around quick," Julian noted.

"Of course he did. He wants to dive into this chocolate booty, and I'm not going to deny him at all. So that means, you gotta go." Lamar looked at his watch. "I have exactly fifty one minutes to clean up and get ready for my man."

"You're kicking me out over some dick."

"Hell, yeah! It's nothing personal. You know, I love you, boo."

Julian shook his head, and got up from the sofa. "I'll talk to you later."

"I'll call you, and let you know how it was," Lamar said, excitedly.

They walked to the front door, and hugged.

"Have fun, be safe, and don't forget what I told you. He might be trouble," Julian stressed.

"He's not going to be any trouble, so go," said Lamar.

Julian left the house. Lamar closed the door, and leaned against it, smiling wickedly.

✠

Lamar only had four minutes before Nafiq's anticipated arrival. In the background, a CD compilation of house music played while Lamar continued to straighten up the house. He walked along the fireplace mantel, quickly taking down numerous photographs of himself. There were shots of Lamar in various vogue poses at a Ball; of Lamar, at one of his more recent exclusively male parties, dancing; and, of Lamar, dressed up as Toni Braxton, for Halloween. He desperately wanted to gain Nafiq's interest, and believed that he had to appear as masculine as possible. Otherwise, he would scare Nafiq away.

Lamar had finished taking down the last photograph when the doorbell rang. Lamar hurriedly turned off the house music, put on some upbeat R&B, and rushed into the hallway, placing the photographs in the closet.

Outside, Nafiq stood to the side of the door, hiding from the illumination of the porch light. His hoodie and winter hat practically hid his face. He nervously looked around as if someone were following or watching him.

Lamar opened the door. "Hi, come in."

Nafiq entered the house, looking around, trying to see if anyone else were present. They walked into the living room. There were snacks on the table. Omarion played on the stereo.

Nafiq stopped, and stood in the middle of the floor.

"Have a seat. Relax," Lamar politely instructed.

Nafiq took a seat on the sofa.

"Do you want something to drink?" asked Lamar.

"Naw. I'm cool."

"You sure?" asked Lamar.

"Yeah, I'm sure."

Lamar nodded, and walked into the kitchen to get himself some soda.

As Lamar prepared a drink for himself, Nafiq looked around the living room, extremely nervous. He thought that this visit would be fun and exciting, but he was again having second thoughts. He had a burning sensation in his stomach. Was he making the right decision? What if someone saw him come to Lamar's house? What if Lamar had a webcam? How would he explain being in Lamar's company?

Nafiq noticed a stack of CDs near the stereo, and decided to check them out. He walked over to the stereo, and started to look at the CD collection. Martha Wash. Sylvester. Kevin Aviance. House remixes to Deborah Cox and Whitney Houston. And the list went on. Nafiq frowned up his face. Nothing but gay music, he thought to himself.

Lamar returned to the living room, and saw Nafiq evaluating his CD collection.

"You see anything you wanna hear?" Lamar asked.

"Naw, I'm straight," Nafiq responded as he walked back to the couch, and took a seat.

Lamar sat on the couch, and turned the music off with a

remote control. He turned on the basketball game with another remote control. Nafiq started to watch the game.

Lamar smiled at Nafiq. "Ya know, I just started getting into basketball."

"Really? What sparked your interest?"

Lamar smiled slyly. "I just think it's an interesting game to follow."

Nafiq nodded. "You play any sports?"

Lamar took a few sips of his drink; then, licked his lips seductively. "No. I just like going out and having fun. Living life to the fullest."

"I feel you," Nafiq replied, trying not to acknowledge Lamar's suggestiveness.

Nafiq refocused his attention on the basketball game, trying to avoid eye contact and any lengthy conversation with Lamar.

Lamar watched Nafiq from the corner of his eye, studying him closely. He hoped Nafiq would make a move. Lamar's body was tense and warm. He was horny as Hell. He needed to feel Nafiq's touch NOW!

Suddenly, Nafiq became excited. He pointed at the TV screen where a basketball player made a three-pointer. "Walker" and the number "9" appeared on the back of the player's jersey. Nafiq jumped up.

"Yeah!" Nafiq loudly cheered. "Dennis Walker is the man."

"Karim Hall is good, too," said Lamar

"Naw. He's pitiful," Nafiq rebutted. "Walker is,

undeniably, one of the best players in the NBA."

"Whatever."

Nafiq continued to focus on the basketball game.

On the television, Walker performed another dramatic move.

Nafiq jumped up again and cheered.

"Do you keep up with the players?" asked Lamar.

"What do you mean?"

"Their personal lives, interests. Stuff like that."

"Yeah."

"Then, I guess you heard about Walker."

Nafiq turned to Lamar, interested.

"What about him?"

"He messes around," Lamar said, emphatically.

"Tell me something new. I'm sure a lot of guys in the NBA cheat on their ladies."

"Obviously, but Walker cheats on his lady with guys."

Nafiq turned to face the TV. However, he wasn't focusing on the game anymore. He was bothered and uncomfortable.

"That's not cool. You shouldn't even joke like that."

"I'm not jokin'. There are a lot of guys, especially sports stars, who are on the DL. That shouldn't be a surprise to anyone."

"Okay, but I'm not really feelin' this conversation or topic. Let's just watch the game."

Lamar gently rubbed Nafiq's inner thigh. "I'm sorry."

Nafiq looked down at Lamar's hand on his thigh. "Yo, what are you doin'?"

Lamar moved his hand closer to Nafiq's crotch, and felt his growing erection through his jeans. "That's what I'm doin'," Lamar said.

He leaned in to kiss Nafiq on the lips, but Nafiq jumped up from the couch, and grabbed his coat and hat.

Lamar stood up, too. "What's wrong?"

Nafiq put on his coat, and walked out of the living room without responding. Lamar followed.

Nafiq stood at the front door, waiting for Lamar to unlock it and to let him out.

"Nafiq, what's wrong?"

"You disrespected me. I didn't ask you to touch me… anywhere."

"I apologize. I didn't mean to make you feel uncomfortable," said Lamar.

Lamar looked Nafiq in the eyes, intently. Nafiq, unnerved, averted his eyes.

Lamar moved closer to Nafiq, and started to massage Nafiq's shoulder. "Relax. You don't have to pretend around me."

Nafiq quickly moved his shoulder away. "Let me out!" he demanded.

Lamar unlocked the door, and Nafiq immediately walked out of the house without saying goodbye. Lamar closed the door, disappointed and saddened, once again.

CHAPTER 5

The warm shower water fell upon Nafiq's naked body as he turned around, slowly rinsing the soap suds from his skin. He then reached for the faucet and turned off the water. Nafiq grabbed his soft cotton towel from the towel rack and began to dry his body. He wrapped the towel around his waist, and stepped out of the tub, walking a few steps to the sink. He wiped the fogged mirror with his hand, and stood, looking at himself, frowning. He was getting ready for Kim's house party, but he didn't want to go.

Nafiq left the bathroom and walked to his bedroom. He closed the door behind him, and took a seat at his desk with his towel hugging his waist. It was 6:41 in the evening, and he had some time to kill before meeting up with Shawn and Jayson.

He turned on the computer, and logged onto his favorite Philly chat group hosted by www.4myniggaz.com. His screen name was youngphilaboi. Nafiq noticed that anaconda, a fellow chatter, was online. He decided to type something:

> **youngphilaboi:** *sup?*
>
> **anaconda:** *chillin'. waitin for one of my bois to pick me up. we goin' to this new club downtown called da hang suite. what 'bout u?*
>
> **youngphilaboi:** *i'm supposed to be goin' to some party around my way, but i ain't really feelin' that.*
>
> **anaconda:** *why don't you check out da hang suite? i can meet you there. we been talkin' online for weeks. maybe we should finally meet.*

Nafiq hesitated. He didn't know how to respond. He's been chatting online for weeks with many people, but has never met them in person. In fact, this is the first time anyone has ever suggested meeting up. He hasn't even exchanged pics online with anyone.

> **youngphilaboi:** *i don't know.*
>
> **anaconda:** *it'll be aight. i won't bite…unless you want me to. :-)*
>
> **youngphilaboi:** *how will I know it's you in the club?*
>
> **anaconda:** *i'm dark-skinned, and have short, black, wavy hair. i'm 5'9", attractive. i'm wearing a blue, Rocawear jump suit with gray Timbs, and a silver chain with my name- Terrence. so u down?*

Terrence's description didn't seem bad. Nafiq was definitely interested now.

> **youngphilaboi:** *where's the spot?*
> **anaconda:** *it's in north philly. in an alley between 10th and callowhill.*
> **youngphilaboi:** *is it discreet?*
> **anaconda:** *hell yeah. i'm not trying to put myself out there like dat. u feel me?*
> **youngphilaboi:** *true... u need id?*
> **anaconda:** *naw. as long as you a true brotha and not a fem or fatty it's all good. they got blunts, dollar drinks, and, of course, hot thugged-out niggas like me. u can't go wrong. it's gonna be off da hook.*

Nafiq smiled to himself. He continued to type.

> **youngphilaboi:** *aight. i'll come and check you out.*
> **anaconda:** *cool. i should be there around 11:00.*
> **youngphilaboi:** *aight. see you.*
> **anaconda:** *peace.*

Nafiq logged out of the chat group, and sat at his computer, briefly weighing his options, which wasn't too difficult for him. He got out of his seat, and walked over to the nightstand where his cellphone sat. He picked up the cellphone, and dialed Shawn's number. Shawn picked up.

"Yo, I'll be over in a half," Shawn quickly said.

"There's been a change of plans."

"What you talkin' 'bout?"

"Family emergency. My aunt's really sick, and me and my family have to drive to Delaware in a few minutes."

"You playin' wit me, right?"

"Naw."

"You can't get out of it?" Shawn asked.

"Man, come on. It's my mom's sister. She's sick," asserted Nafiq.

"This is real fucked up. Kim and Janet are expecting me and you at the party. We supposed to be a team."

"Yo, I'm sorry, but I can't go."

"Aight, man. I'll holla at you later," Shawn said before slamming down the phone.

Nafiq frowned for a quick moment, upset about deceiving Shawn and disappointing him, but when Nafiq envisioned himself parting at Da Hang Suite, his spirits were instantly lifted.

He threw his cellphone onto the bed, and put on his new Sean Jean striped, polo shirt, jeans, and Air Force Ones. He carefully tied a do-rag over his braids, and splashed on some cologne. He looked in the full-length mirror at himself, critiquing his appearance and adjusting what he didn't like. He looked in the mirror again, and cocked his chin with satisfaction. He was ready.

Nafiq headed downstairs to the living room where Reginald and Gwendolyn were watching an old blaxploitation flick. Nafiq walked over to them.

"I'm going to Kim's party now. I'll see you later."

BREATHE

"Enjoy yourself," said Reginald.

"Have fun, and remember you need to be back home by 12:30. I don't want you to be too tired for Sunday service," said Gwendolyn.

Nafiq frowned at the curfew time. "All right."

Nafiq walked out the living room, and grabbed his coat, hat, and gloves from the hallway closet. He put them on and left the house.

On the porch, Nafiq stood, and looked at the clear sky and bright, full moon. He smiled. He had never been to a gay or bisexual club before, and Da Hang Suite sounded enticing. The club was also discreet, which was his primary incentive for going. Nafiq was finally ready to check out the scene and explore the nightlife. He was ready to hang with brothas like himself.

✠

After getting lost, Nafiq finally arrived at the corner of 10th and Callowhill. He took out a piece of paper to double check the address of Da Hang Suite, and put the paper back into his pocket. He walked up to the front of a large, dilapidated building that looked abandoned. Hip-hop music filtered through the doorway. A short, stocky doorman stood in front of the entrance. He motioned for Nafiq to enter.

Nafiq walked up to a Plexiglas window.

"Ten," said the man behind the window.

Nafiq slid a $10 bill under the window.

"Step over there," the man behind the window commanded, expressionless, his head motioning to the right side of the window.

The bouncers, huge, 6'6" thuggish men with businesslike demeanors, searched Nafiq for weapons. Nafiq was shocked by the forceful search procedure. Satisfied, the bouncers motioned for him to enter.

Nafiq eased into the main club area, and looked around in amazement. The room was filled with a thick, smoky haze. The potent smell of marijuana filled the air as people passed around their blunts.

T.I. blared through the speakers. A stripper, partially dressed in black ninja gear, gesticulated on an elevated platform. Nafiq looked up at the DJ, who was mixing on another elevated platform. The DJ booth and its surrounding area were decorated with blue and white blinking Christmas lights.

Nafiq spotted an empty table on the other side of the room, and started his trek toward the table. As Nafiq pushed through the large, crowded dance floor, which was filled mostly with teenagers and guys in their twenties and early thirties, eyes fell upon him. They had detected fresh meat.

On his way across the dance floor, Nafiq accidentally bumped into a tall, skinny kid who was staring at himself in a large wall mirror as he vogued exuberantly. The kid wore a flashy, colorful shirt with rhinestones embroidered on the front.

"Watch where the fuck you're goin', bitch!" the kid said

with hostile intent.

Nafiq stopped, and glared at him. The kid stopped dancing, and reciprocated the glare. Nafiq's face turned angry and intimidating. He was ready to fuck kid up.

Not wanting to aggravate the situation, the kid smacked his lips, cut his eyes, and resumed his dancing.

Nafiq continued his walk, and arrived at the table. He took a seat, and looked at his watch. It was 11:07. Nafiq started observing the environment as he scoped the area for his online buddy, Terrence (a.k.a. anaconda).

Not more than a minute later, Nafiq caught the eye of Chris, a young brotha in his late twenties. Chris had a brown complexion and a smooth, bald head. His designer frames made him look astute yet sexy. Chris smiled, and Nafiq nodded. Chris winked, and Nafiq smiled shyly. Chris got up from his table, and walked over to Nafiq.

Chris casually motioned to the empty seat across from Nafiq. "May I?"

"Sure."

Chris sat down, and extended his right hand for a shake. "Chris."

Nafiq shook Chris' hand. "Na--" Nafiq stopped himself. "Rick."

"Nice name. It suits you," said Chris, smirking.

Nafiq nodded.

"Would you like a drink, Rick?" asked Chris.

"Naw, I'm cool," Nafiq replied.

"Here with your boyfriend?"

Nafiq looked stunned by the question. "No."

"An attractive, young brotha like yourself doesn't have a boyfriend? That's hard to believe," Chris said, acting surprised.

Nafiq shook his head.

Chris moved in closer. "You want one?"

Nafiq moved away, surprised by Chris' forwardness. He didn't respond.

As he lifted his bottle of Corona with lime, Chris took a sip and asked, "Do you like movies?"

"Yeah."

"Cool. Why don't we head over to my place? I have a real nice condo a few blocks away. It's a lot more comfortable than this place. We can watch some movies on my flat screen, and get to know each other a little better. You feel me?"

Chris grabbed Nafiq's hand, and started to softly rub Nafiq's inner palm with the tips of his fingers. Nafiq pulled his hand away.

"I'm sorry, but-"

"What's the matter?" asked Chris with an annoyed look on his face.

"Nothing's the matter. I just want to sit here for a bit and chill. Plus, I'm waiting on a friend."

"Oh, okay. I'll let you wait for your friend. Talk to you later."

"Aight."

Chris got up from the table, disgusted, and walked to the other side of the club. He started flirting with another young kid.

Nafiq shook his head, and checked his watch again. It was now 11:31 and still no sign of someone who resembled Terrence's description. Nafiq frowned. He couldn't believe that he was possibly being stood up. However, Nafiq tried not to be fazed, and continued observing the surroundings, determined to enjoy himself tonight.

As he scoped the club again, he saw Lamar and Julian enter. He instantly became nervous, and turned away, trying not to be seen. However, Lamar, observing the surroundings as well, recognized Nafiq's profile. Lamar excitedly tapped Julian on the shoulder.

"Oh, my God. Nafiq's here."

Lamar nodded his head in the direction Nafiq was sitting.

Julian looked at Nafiq, recognizing him.

Lamar grabbed Julian's arm. "Let's go over and say 'Hi.'"

Nafiq saw Lamar and Julian approaching him, and grew increasingly nervous.

"What's up?" asked Lamar.

"Chillin'" responded Nafiq.

"This is my friend, Julian," Lamar introduced.

Nafiq nodded his head. "Wassup?"

"Hi," said Julian.

Suddenly, the music abruptly stopped. Everyone stopped talking, and faced the center of the dance floor. Five seconds later, a flamboyantly dressed drag queen cartwheeled to the center of the dance floor. A house remix to Cheryl Lynn's "Got To Be Real" started playing, and the drag queen started lip-syncing to the song. Many of the club patrons clapped, and waved their hands in the air, supporting "Miss Godiva."

Nafiq was repulsed by the sight of the drag queen, and appalled at the club for being a fraud. The club wasn't a DL spot, but a place filled with voguing fems, wanna-be hard niggas, and wanna-be females.

"That is my girl. She is fierce. Come on. Let's get closer," Lamar said as he moved closer to see Miss Godiva perform.

Nafiq didn't move. He stared in disgust.

"Do you want to move closer?" asked Julian.

"Hell, no!" Nafiq shouted.

Julian playfully laughed. "I guess, this isn't your cup of tea?"

"No, but it's all good. I'm 'bout to roll out anyway. I'm not really feelin' this."

"Why? What's wrong?"

"The people. The environment."

"What's wrong with the people and the environment? You know what type of club you're in, right?"

Silence prevailed for a few seconds. Nafiq responded, "I know where I am. It's too… gay for me, and I'm ready to go."

At that instance, Miss Godiva finished her fabulous performance, bowing and blowing airborne kisses to the audience as she received praise. "I love you back," she shouted to everyone.

Soon afterwards, a reggae jam started playing.

"Ohhh… This is the song. Let's dance," suggested Julian.

"Naw. I need to go."

"This can be your farewell dance. Come on."

"Naw!"

Julian playfully pouted. "Please…"

Julian was too cute. His dimples showed and his beautiful, bright eyes twinkled. Nafiq smiled. He couldn't resist.

"Aight. Then, I'm out."

Julian danced out onto the crowded dance floor, and motioned for Nafiq to come join him. They started to dance, and seemed to be having genuine fun. There was a pure and magnetic energy between them.

At the bar, Lamar sat on the bar stool, chatting and laughing it up with Miss Godiva. She looked in the direction of the dance floor, and tapped Lamar on the shoulder.

"Ooohh, chile. Look at the brotha Julian's dancing with."

Lamar looked, and quickly frowned.

"Julian always pulls the phine ass guys," said Miss Godiva.

Lamar took a heavy shot of rum, and glared at the two. His eyes burned through them. His body seethed with anger.

✠

The farewell dance had turned into several non-stop dances. Nafiq and Julian were happily dancing the night away until Miss Godiva sashayed up to them.

"Julian, I think Lamar's ready to go home. He's tore up, honey."

Julian and Nafiq turned to look at Lamar.

Lamar, slouched to the side, took another shot, staring with a malevolent gaze at Julian and Nafiq.

Miss Godiva flirtatiously smiled at Nafiq, and blew a kiss to him. "Hi."

Julian sighed, and walked toward the bar where Lamar sat. Nafiq followed, ignoring Miss Godiva's advances.

"Did you two enjoy yourselves?" Lamar slurred.

"We had an okay time. Did you?" asked Julian as he reached for the empty, shot glass in Lamar's hand.

Lamar smacked Julian's hand away.

"Of course, I did. I didn't mind being left out of all the festivities," said Lamar, angrily.

Julian wrapped his arm around Lamar's waist, and tried to lift him from the seat.

"Come on. I'm taking you to my house," said Julian. "Your mom shouldn't be seeing you like this, again."

"Don't touch me," Lamar said, pushing Julian away. "I'm staying right the fuck here."

"Lamar, don't be like this. You're drunk, and making a scene. Besides, the club is about to close soon. It's almost two."

"Almost two," Nafiq panicked. He looked at his watch. It was 1:56. His adrenaline instantly raced. "Yo, I gotta go."

Nafiq rushed out of the club.

"Go ahead. Don't just stand here. Chase after your little boyfriend," Lamar insisted, sarcastically.

"We were just dancing," Julian defended. "It's not even like that."

"Of course not," Lamar said, rolling his eyes.

Julian didn't respond. What could he say? He stood,

frowning to himself and feeling guilty about the entire situation. He knew that Lamar liked Nafiq, but his dances with Nafiq were intended to be innocent. Little did he expect that he would enjoy Nafiq's company as much as he did.

✠

A jitney cab pulled up to the curb in front of the Johnson house. Nafiq paid the driver, and stepped out of the black 1989 Ford Taurus. He stared at the house. All of the lights were turned out. Nafiq flashed a smile of relief, and quietly headed toward the front door, trying not to make much noise in the snow. He took out his key, opened the front door, and tiptoed into the house. Suddenly, the living room light flashed on. Nafiq peeked into the room, and saw Gwendolyn and Reginald sitting on the sofa, waiting.

"Nafiq, get in here!" Gwendolyn yelled, angrily.

Nafiq slowly walked into the living room, and stood in front of his parents.

"Have a seat," said Reginald.

Nafiq took a seat across from them, his hands clasped in his lap.

"Look at the clock," said Gwendolyn.

"I know-"

"I said look at the clock, boy," Gwendolyn said with authority in her voice.

Nafiq looked at the clock on the wall.

"What time is it?" asked Gwendolyn.

"A quarter 'till three."

"And what time were you supposed to be home?" asked Gwendolyn.

"12:30."

"Is there any particular reason why you're over two hours late?" Gwendolyn asked.

"I lost track of time."

"Did you also lose your mind? You couldn't call?" asked Gwendolyn.

"I forgot my cellphone here."

"That's no excuse," said Reginald. "You could have used Shawn's cellphone or called from the party."

"Whenever you hang out with Shawn or Jayson, there's always a problem," said Gwendolyn. "They're hoodlums and bad influences."

"I'm sorry," apologized Nafiq.

"And what high school party lasts until three in the morning?" huffed Gwendolyn, displeased. She looked at Nafiq, continuing. "Was there even parental supervision?"

"Yes," replied Nafiq.

"Nevertheless, this is unacceptable. Tomorrow, I want that girl's number who hosted the party. We need to have a talk with her parents. You-all aren't grown yet," snapped Gwendolyn.

A look of panic covered Nafiq's face. "But mom-"

"Nafiq, go ahead to bed. We have church in the morning," said Reginald.

Nafiq got up from his chair, and left the room.

Gwendolyn and Reginald traded skeptical glances.

"This isn't like Nafiq. I don't know what to think," said Gwendolyn.

Reginald nodded in agreement.

✠

Inside his room, Nafiq lay motionless on his bed, fully dressed, his eyes wide open. Moonlight flooded the room with a foreboding luminance.

CHAPTER 6

It was Sunday morning. Churchgoers entered the Temple of Truth AME Church and walked down the aisles, taking their seats and chatting. The vast majority of members were dressed in elegant splendor. The older women wore stylish, double-breasted suits, and donned matching crowns while the younger females wore pretty, respectable dresses. The men and boys sported tailored suits, which varied in color from absolute granite black to pastel green. The sanctuary could have doubled as a fashion consortium.

In the front of the sanctuary, the Johnson family sat together, talking and waiting for the service to commence.

Like clockwork, at 11 o'clock, the pianist began to play an

up tempo, gospel song, silencing the church conversations. Soon afterwards, Kiara walked up to the front of the church, took the microphone, and began to sing "Your Name Is Jesus." The congregation joined in, waving and shouting. They were hyped up, and helped Kiara and the choir turn the song out. Once Kiara finished belting her heart out, she left the floor, and sat with the rest of her family.

Reverend Douglas, a 6'5" burly, austere looking man, walked to the pulpit. The entire church was silent.

Reverend Douglas began speaking in a strong, deliberate tone.

"Good mornin', my brothas and sistas. We're fortunate on this day, to be amongst each other to pay respect and honor to the Lord Jesus Christ. We're also here, today, as the Lord has directed me, to address an important and controversial topic: Homosexuality in the African-American community."

Nafiq looked as if his heart skipped a few beats.

"Before I begin, let us refer to Leviticus chapter 18 verse 22. Say 'Amen' when you find it."

A series of "Amens" came from the congregation.

"You shall not lie with a male as with a woman; such a thing is an abomination. You shall not have carnal relations with an animal, defiling yourself with it. May the Lord add a blessing to the reading of His Word."

The congregation shouted "Amen."

Reverend Douglas continued. "Folks, there has been a lie making its way throughout this country. This lie is corrupting the minds of our nation, our children, and our very race. This lie suggests that being gay is cool, trendy, and acceptable. It's okay to be gay."

A female churchgoer shouted, "It's a sin."

"Books, affirming homosexuality, appear in our libraries. Books that our own children can easily take out and read. Gay characters even appear on primetime television. But I'm here to tell you. God hates all workers of iniquity. Can I hear another Amen?"

The congregation shouted "Amen." A few members, including Gwendolyn, stood up, waiving their Bibles in the air, shouting "Preach, Reverend."

Nafiq sat, frozen, with sadness on his face.

Reverend Douglas continued to preach for what seemed like eternity to Nafiq, but was only forty-five minutes. He addressed everything from the fall of sodomy laws to the legalization of gay marriage; from the "new" DL phenomenon to how homosexuality is a product of white racism used to destroy the black man and the black family.

Nafiq looked around, watching the riled-up congregation. They listened attentively, absorbing every word.

The Reverend concluded, "The only hope that homosexuals have is to have the unambiguous Truth preached to them. And, perhaps, God will soften their hearts, and grant them repentance to depart from their abominable sin. If these degenerates, these sodomites fail to abide by God's Word, there is a Hell for them. A Hell where all impenitent sinners will reside for eternity. Can I hear an Amen, my brothas and sistas?"

The entire congregation erupted with a thunderous "Amen." They stood up, and frantically waived their Bibles in the air, shouting "Sin is sin! There is a Hell for them!"

The choir rose, and Kiara returned. The choir started to joyously sing and clap. The congregation joined in with the same vibrant energy of the choir.

Nafiq swayed to the music, halfheartedly.

✠

Nafiq, dressed in his church clothes, walked into his room, and collapsed onto the bed. He thought about the sermon, about the fiery words, and about how bad it made him feel. He felt low and despicable. However, the Reverend's words didn't convince Nafiq to avail himself and to "depart from [his] abominable sin." Instead, it forced him to think of new ways to further smother himself in darkness. To become more skilled and crafty at hiding his true self.

After a half hour of gradually plunging into a deep depression, there was a knock at the door.

Nafiq sat up. "Come in," he said, somberly.

Reginald walked into the room, and closed the door behind himself. He took a seat next to Nafiq on his bed.

"I want to talk to you."

Nafiq looked at Reginald, attentive and nervous.

"Your mother and I are very upset and disappointed by what happened last night. You've never exhibited this type of behavior before? What's going on?"

"Nothing, Dad. I didn't mean to violate my curfew. I was just having fun, and lost track of time."

"You could have called at some point, though."

"I'm sorry. I wasn't thinking, but it won't happen again."

"I know it won't, but I'm still going to need that girl's number who hosted the party."

"Dad, please... That's going to be embarrassing. I promise this won't happen, again," Nafiq pleaded.

Reginald looked at Nafiq, and saw the sincerity in his eyes.

"Okay. I'll overlook the situation this time, but you've been forewarned," Reginald said, sternly.

"All right," Nafiq acknowledged.

Reginald rose from the bed. "I'll talk to your mother. Also, I need you to pick up some clipper blades for me from the mall before it closes. When you come downstairs, I'll give you the money."

"Okay."

Reginald left the room.

Nafiq breathed a sigh of relief.

✠

After picking up his father's clipper blades from the barber supply store, Nafiq walked around the mall, checking out the CD stores and shoe stores, trying to get his mind off of the past 24 hours. Before going to the subway stop to go home, he decided to use one of the mall's department store restrooms.

As Nafiq entered the restroom, he instantly frowned his nose up at the distinct, acrid smell of urine and disinfectant cleanser, which penetrated the air.

Nafiq walked past the urinals, which were occupied by four guys, two of whom were teenagers. He noticed that their hands were moving as if they were masturbating. He looked again, and realized that was exactly what they were doing. Their shafts were, long, hard, and throbbing. They gave Nafiq a nod as they stroked away. Nafiq's eyes bulged with shock.

Nafiq continued to walk toward the back of the restroom where the stalls were located. He observed closely. He was appalled at what was going on, but, at the same time, he was curious. He had never witnessed something like this before; nor had he known that such things took place. Nafiq turned the corner, and saw a group of five good-looking African-American men huddled in a close circle. Three of the men's backs were turned away from Nafiq. They were masturbating together, too.

As Nafiq observed, the three men began to move back to reveal a man in a navy-blue business suit having unprotected, anal sex with a young boy in his late teens. It was Alonzo! Alonzo held onto the boy's waist as he rammed into him. Nafiq and Alonzo's eyes met. Nafiq was frozen in place-stunned, confused, saddened, frightened, angry. He felt the full gamut of emotions. Alonzo was surprised for a brief moment, but turned his head as if he didn't see Nafiq.

Nafiq rushed out of the restroom and stopped. He hyperventilated. He couldn't believe what he had seen. He would have never fathomed Alonzo messing around. He especially couldn't believe that Alonzo was cheating on his sister.

After a few minutes, Nafiq was able to regain his composure. He picked up his pace on his way to the subway stop.

✠

In the Johnson house, Gwendolyn hummed Deniece Williams' "God Is Truly Amazing" as she carefully arranged the plush pillows on the sofa. She was straightening up for the family's traditional Sunday dinner. As Gwendolyn worked happily but intently, Nafiq entered the house and walked into the living room.

"Hi, Nafiq. You need to go freshen up for dinner. Kiara, Alonzo, and Marcus will be here soon."

"Okay," Nafiq said.

He began to ascend the stairs, but before he reached the top, the doorbell rang.

Gwendolyn walked into the hallway, and answered the door. She was greeted by Alonzo.

"Hi, Mom," said Alonzo. He gave Gwendolyn a peck on the cheek, and followed her into the living room.

"Where's Kiara?" Gwendolyn inquired.

"She's on her way. I had some business to take care of so

we agreed to meet here."

Alonzo noticed Nafiq standing on the stairs.

"Hey, what's up, Nafiq?" he said, pleasantly.

Nafiq stiffly nodded.

"Well, since you're both here, can you two take the food from the kitchen into the dining room?" Gwendolyn asked. "Everything's already in serving bowls."

"No problem," responded Alonzo.

Nafiq descended the stairs, and entered the kitchen with Alonzo. Alonzo walked to the kitchen table. Nafiq walked to the stove and stood; his eyes stared with disdain.

"How could you do this to my sister?"

"Man, mind your business."

"My sister is my business."

"She may be your sister, but she's my woman. She's my responsibility. I look out for her now."

"How are you looking out for her? You're cheating on her with dudes... in a restroom. Are you trying to give her a disease or something?"

Alonzo walked up to Nafiq. They stood eye to eye.

"Mind your damn business. What I do in my life is my business. If I want to fuck another guy, wherever, I can and will," Alonzo said in a hushed yet aggressive voice.

"You're foul."

"And you have a lot to learn. I urge you to shut your face. Otherwise, you'll regret it."

"You're threatening me now?"

"Nafiq, you need to deal with your own issues before you

involve yourself in someone else's. You have more at risk than
I do."

"How is that?"

"Philly is small, and people talk. And everyone has seen
you talking to that dirty, black faggot. What's his name? Lamar.
Didn't you go over his house, too?"

Nafiq was shocked.

"People are starting to wonder about you," Alonzo said,
smirking. "If you want to survive in this world, you need to
learn how to play the game. Don't be a fool. Keep your shit
discreet."

Alonzo winked at Nafiq, and left the kitchen, carrying a
tray of food.

Nafiq clenched his teeth.

✠

The Johnson family sat at the large, mahogany dinner
table, which was covered with delicious, homemade foods:
baked macaroni-and-cheese, fresh collard greens, meaty sirloin
steaks, garlic and herb mashed potatoes with gravy, golden-
brown buttermilk biscuits, and sparkling apple cider. Everyone
was chatting, and enjoying the food. Kiara sat between Alonzo
and Nafiq.

"You've truly outdone yourself this time. This meal
surpasses delicious," Alonzo told Gwendolyn.

"Thank you," said Gwendolyn, smiling, moved by
Alonzo's compliment.

"So how's the job?" Reginald asked Alonzo.

"It's great. As a matter of fact, I was promoted to VP of A&R on Friday."

"Congratulations," said Reginald.

Gwendolyn and Marcus congratulated Alonzo as well.

Nafiq stared daggers at Alonzo as he picked at his food.

Kiara smiled proudly. Her man was making moves. Climbing the corporate ladder. Shattering that glass ceiling. And she was there to support and love him along the way.

Gwendolyn faced Alonzo. "Why are you just telling us the good news now? Aren't you a couple days late?"

"We wanted to wait for the right time to tell you," said Kiara.

"A right time?" asked Marcus.

"Yeah. Kiara and I are moving to New York City. Triple-P is expanding, and the new main office is going to be located in Manhattan," Alonzo declared.

"What about your boutique?" asked Reginald, a little concerned.

"I'm going to open up a new boutique in New York. It's a wonderful market for both of us," said Kiara.

"Congratulations to both of you. I'm sure this will be a great opportunity," said Gwendolyn.

"Thank you," Alonzo responded, "but I have another special surprise."

Alonzo reached into his pants pocket. Everyone stopped eating and looked at Alonzo. He took out a silver case, and kneeled on the floor beside Kiara. He opened the case, and revealed a platinum diamond ring, which sparkled in the light. Gwendolyn and Kiara looked at each other, excited. Marcus and Reginald smiled. Nafiq looked apoplectic.

"Kiara, you are the love and joy of my life. You are truly my soulmate. You've changed my life in so many positive ways, and I can't think of myself living a day without you. So I ask, would you do me the honor of taking my hand in marriage?"

Tears fell from Kiara's eyes. "Yes, baby, yes! I love you."

Alonzo slid the ring onto Kiara's finger, and they hugged and kissed. Everyone, except Nafiq, congratulated them.

Reginald rose from the table. "I'll get the champagne."

Kiara turned to Nafiq, and hugged him tightly.

"Congratulations," Nafiq said, solemnly.

✠

After Sunday dinner, Nafiq walked Kiara to Alonzo's car. Kiara beamed with happiness.

"Fiq, I can't believe it. I'm finally going to be Mrs. Kiara Miller."

Kiara looked at her ring, and showed Nafiq.

"And look at this ring. It's unbelievable."

"It's nice," said Nafiq, somberly.

"What's wrong? You're happy for me, right?"

"I just had too much to eat. Indigestion."

Alonzo walked out of the house and toward the car. He kissed Kiara on her lips.

"All right, all right. Break it up. Time to go home," said Alonzo.

Kiara gave Nafiq a big hug. "Bye."

"Peace," Nafiq said.

"See you later," Alonzo told Nafiq.

Nafiq stared angrily. He didn't respond.

Alonzo and Kiara got into the car, and drove off. Nafiq watched the black Mercedes Benz fade into the cold, empty night.

✠

Inside her apartment, Kiara stood in front of the mirrored closet door, smiling anxiously. She was excited about her engagement to Alonzo, and envisioned herself in full wedding raiment and accessories at the future ceremony...

She stood in the rose petal strewn aisle in her elegant, white, floral-lace fishtail gown, which gently swayed in the soft spring breeze. Birds chirped merrily. The sweet fragrance of flowers filled the air. The familiar chords of Felix Mendelssohn's "The Wedding March" played in the background.

Alonzo walked toward Kiara from behind in his black, double-breasted tuxedo. Kiara waited with anticipation as he approached. Finally, standing next to each other, the priest began to administer the sacred vows, which would solidify their eternal and holy union forever.

CHAPTER 7

Gwendolyn sat at the kitchen table, reading the latest edition of *Essence* magazine and drinking her coffee.

Nafiq walked in, carrying his book bag.

"Good morning, Mom," he said as he grabbed a banana from the fruit basket on the counter, and put it into his book bag.

"Aren't you going to eat breakfast?" asked Gwendolyn.

"I don't have time. I have a meeting with the coach."

Gwendolyn looked at Nafiq, concerned.

"Is everything all right?"

"Yeah. We're just discussing the upcoming game."

"I was talking about things in general. You haven't

seemed like yourself for a few days."

"Everything is cool." Nafiq quickly changed the subject. "Off today?"

"I am, but I'm going to help your Dad with the books for this month," Gwendolyn replied.

"Cool."

Nafiq walked to Gwendolyn, and gave her a kiss on the forehead. "I'll see you later."

"Have a good day at school."

Gwendolyn watched Nafiq rush out of the kitchen. She continued to look concerned.

✠

Coach Franklin sat at his desk reading *The Philadelphia Inquirer*. Behind him, trophies and 8x10 photographs of former Central athletes, some of which have played at major colleges and/or in the NBA, filled the bookshelves and walls. On another wall, a bulletin board with daily reminders and team schedules hung.

Nafiq entered the office. Coach Franklin put down his paper, and motioned for Nafiq to have a seat.

"Do you know why I asked you to come see me, Nafiq?"

"No, Coach."

"To be quite honest, your game has been progressively slipping for the past few weeks."

Nafiq was stunned by Coach Franklin's observation.

"Is there anything going on that may be affecting your

performance?"

"No, Coach. Not at all."

"How's your family?"

"Everyone's good. Everything's good."

Coach looked at Nafiq with suspicious eyes.

"I also think you should know that, during a faculty meeting last week, I got chewed out by your Calculus, History, and English teachers. They accused me of working you too hard, and that's why your A's in the classes have suddenly plummeted to C's. The ironic thing is, I haven't been working you that hard."

"C's," Nafiq mumbled to himself, disappointed.

"Apparently, you didn't get your mid-report grades yet."

Nafiq sighed deeply. "No, Coach, I haven't."

"This is all to say that there is something wrong, and it's greatly affecting your academics and athletic performance. You've always been a straight-A student, and you've consistently been an outstanding player. You're also like a son to me, Nafiq. If there is something wrong, please don't be shy about coming to me."

"Thank you, Coach, but there's nothing wrong. Just an aberration. You don't have to worry."

"I hope so, because the championship game is in a few weeks. If your game isn't back to where it needs to be, and, soon, I'm going to bench you."

"But the recruiter from Duke will be there."

"But if you're not playing your best game and giving your maximum, then what's the point? You don't only reflect poorly on yourself, you reflect poorly on the team."

Nafiq frowned. "I understand. May I go now?"

"Yes."

Nafiq got up from the chair and left the office, closing the door behind him. He walked down the hallway toward his locker, distraught. Julian saw Nafiq, and walked up to him. They struggled through the crowded hallway together.

"How've you been? I tried calling you, but Lamar gave me the wrong number."

Nafiq didn't respond.

Julian noticed that Nafiq appeared very upset.

"Are you okay?"

"I actually want you to leave me alone. Aight? And I want you to tell your boi, Lamar, the same thing. Don't ever come near me again."

Julian was taken aback by Nafiq's demeanor and response. He frowned. "Okay."

Julian walked away.

Nafiq leaned against his locker, saddened.

Shawn and Jayson, who were watching the brief exchange between Nafiq and Julian from afar, looked at each other with an expression of contempt and anger.

✠

In the family room at the Johnson house, Gwendolyn turned on the computer and inserted a floppy disk into the A:/ drive. She typed something, and the monitor displayed numerous indecipherable characters. Gwendolyn sighed, and typed something again. Still indecipherable characters. A look of frustration grew on her face. She took her disk out of the computer, and left the room.

Gwendolyn went to Nafiq's room, took a seat at his desk, and turned his computer on. She inserted the disk, and clicked the mouse. Suddenly, on the monitor, an image of a naked Black male popped onto the screen. He lay on a bed, legs spread apart, gripping his thick, 10" manhood tightly. Gwendolyn instantly recoiled, and covered her mouth in disbelief.

She clicked the mouse again, and another naked male image popped up. The male, positioned doggy-style, spread his plump ass apart with his hands, exposing his tight hole. Gwendolyn was taken aback. Way back. She was transfixed for a long time.

She noticed a blinking box at the bottom of the screen, and clicked on it. Suddenly, a nude picture of Lamar, sprawled across his couch, enlarged. A message appeared below the picture: Nafiq, I really like you. Do you forgive me?

Gwendolyn, shocked, stared at the screen and the message. Then, she burst into tears.

✠

In the cafeteria, Nafiq carried his tray of food to the table where Shawn and Jayson were conversing and eating their lunch.

"Yo, what's good?" asked Nafiq.

Shawn and Jayson stopped their conversation, and didn't respond. They continued to eat their lunch, but silently.

Nafiq sat down. "No one can speak?"

"Naw. Not to a fudge-packin' faggot," Jayson blurted.

"Excuse me?"

"You know what Jayson's talking about. Stop frontin'," Shawn said.

"No, I don't. And don't call me a fudge packer or a faggot. Aight?"

"You like hanging around them. I just assumed you were one, too," said Jayson.

"You all are on some other shit right now, and I'm not in the mood," Nafiq said.

Nafiq stood up, and picked up his lunch tray.

"Yo Shawn, he even runs away like a lil' sissy faggot," said Jayson.

"I don't hang with faggots, and I'm not a faggot. So you two obviously got your own issues to resolve."

"We got issues? Who the fuck has two notorious homos hanging at his locker everyday? And when was the last time you were wit a bitch, man," said Shawn.

"We were talking about schoolwork. I guess you wouldn't know anything about that, you retarded bastard."

"What the fuck you call me?" asked Shawn.

Shawn got up from his seat.

"Don't you ever disrespect me," Shawn shouted at Nafiq.

"You disrespect me. I disrespect you," said Nafiq. "So

let's just drop it now. We bois. We fam. It's over. Aight?"

"Fuck that. We ain't shit. And I'm not gonna let some pussy punk talk shit to me." Shawn stepped up to Nafiq. "I should kick your bitch ass across this fuckin' cafeteria?"

"Shawn, you need to have a seat and chill out," Nafiq said.

"Fuck you."

Nafiq's jawbone flexed tensely. He positioned his body in a defensive stance, preparing for what seemed to be an imminent showdown.

Suddenly, Shawn pushed Nafiq back, and swung at Nafiq's face. Nafiq quickly blocked the shot, and punched Shawn in the chest, knocking him back. Shawn rushed Nafiq, and they both fell to the floor, brawling. A large crowd of students ran toward Nafiq and Shawn, encircling them and yelling. Two male teachers tore through the crowd toward Nafiq and Shawn. Nafiq was on top of Shawn, pummeling him in the face.

The teachers finally reached the two, and broke up the fight. One teacher pinned down a thrashing Nafiq while the other teacher escorted Shawn away. Shawn's nose and mouth bled, and his face was severely swollen. Nafiq's eyes were red and watery. He had a medium-size cut above his eyebrow.

"You betta watch your back," yelled Shawn. "It ain't over yet."

Nafiq felt the cut on his face with his finger. He squinted in pain.

✠

Nafiq walked up to the front door of his house. He stopped and peeked at a sealed letter in his bag. The letter, written on Central stationery, was addressed to Gwendolyn and Reginald. The word "SUSPENSION" in large, red letters appeared on the front. He shook his head.

Nafiq took out his keys and opened the door. He entered the hallway, took off his coat and hat, and put his book bag on the floor. He walked into the living room.

Gwendolyn and Reginald entered from the kitchen, and stood in the entryway between the two rooms.

"Nafiq, sit down," Gwendolyn said. Her eyes were red from crying.

Nafiq took a seat on the sofa, looking concerned.

"Mom, what's wrong?"

Reginald abruptly cut in. "Why the Hell are there pictures of naked men on your computer?" he yelled.

Nafiq was stunned.

"Huh? I... I don't know. What are you talking about?"

"Well, they certainly didn't appear there by themselves," said Reginald.

"I haven't seen any pictures like that. Maybe they were part of some virus or something. Maybe it's spam," Nafiq reasoned.

"Cut the bullshit, Nafiq. I checked, and those pictures were downloaded. In fact, you have an entire library of pictures and streaming files stored on your computer, and I want to know why that shit is there," demanded Reginald, his anger growing into rage.

Nafiq grew nervous.

"Not only that, why did that Lamar boy send you a nude photo of himself? Is that who you really went out with last Saturday?" asked Gwendolyn.

"No."

"Don't lie to us," said Gwendolyn. "I ran into that boy's mother at the supermarket yesterday, and she told me everything. I argued with her, denying it, but it looks like I'm the fool. How could you do this to our family?"

Nafiq's throat tightened. He couldn't say a word. His body was tense.

"So tell us. Are you a homosexual? Are you gay?" Reginald asked, his eyes bulging, his throat tensing.

A numbness quickly overcame Nafiq's body, but he quickly answered, "No!"

Gwendolyn stormed out of the living room, and quickly came back with two, hefty garbage bags filled with clothes and other personal items.

"This is a holy house. We will not tolerate this. You are a liar and a sinner. How could you disgrace your family?" said Gwendolyn.

Nafiq looked at the two bags, and stood up. Tears began to well in his eyes.

"Why are you doing this?"

"It's not what we're doing. It's what you're doing. God doesn't approve of it and neither do we. When you change your ways, then we'll let you come back home," asserted Gwendolyn.

"So you're just going to throw me out onto the streets?"

"You should have thought about the consequences a long time ago," said Reginald.

"This is crazy!" Nafiq yelled at his parents.

"Don't raise your voice to me!" Reginald yelled back.

Nafiq kicked over the garbage bags; sending his clothes flying across the floor.

Reginald quickly grabbed Nafiq's throat in a jugoku-jime choke and started cutting off his air.

"Boy, you have some nerve," Reginald said as he choked his son. Nafiq struggled to break free of his father's grasp, but couldn't. Gwendolyn quickly ran up to Reginald, and started to beg her husband to let Nafiq go.

Reginald finally let go of Nafiq's throat, and Nafiq gasped for air. He glared at his mother and father with pain, sadness, and shock in his eyes. He ran out of the front door without his coat or hat, and sprinted down the street to the neighborhood park.

The flickering lights of the street lamps, near the park, illuminated the desolate basketball court. Nafiq stood in the middle of the court before he collapsed onto the ground. His eyes swelled with tears; his body frigid. His knees sunk deep in the snow as he clutched at his head in despair, crying hard. He was traumatized. He couldn't believe that his parents found out his secret. He also couldn't believe his father choked him. And what about his living situation? What about his future?

How was he going to go on with his life being identified as a black, gay man? What about employment? What about finding a place to live? What about basketball? He felt that in a matter of minutes, his life had been irreversibly damaged.

Deeply despondent, Nafiq got up from the ground, and started to walk downtown in the bitter weather, feeling lost and empty. As he wandered among the downtown city-dwellers, sleet and snow fell from the sky, and lodged in his hair. The temperature had dropped tremendously, and Nafiq shivered. His face and hands were cold and red, almost frostbitten. Once he couldn't take the cold weather anymore, he walked into a coffee shop to keep warm.

Nafiq sat down in a booth, and tried to warm himself up. Coincidentally, not far from where Nafiq sat, Julian was drinking espresso and reading a magazine. Julian glanced up, and, instantly, his eyes met with Nafiq's. Julian smiled gently. He was glad to see Nafiq despite their previous encounter. But Nafiq averted his eyes. That's when Julian decided to confront Nafiq. He walked over to Nafiq's booth and sat down. Julian noticed that Nafiq looked extremely forlorn.

"What's wrong? You don't look like yourself," asked Julian.

Nafiq lowered his eyes. He tried to tell Julian, but the words wouldn't come out.

Nafiq tried to speak again. "My parents threw me out."

"What? When did this happen?" he asked.

"A few hours ago."

"I'm sorry. ...Do you have a place to stay?" asked Julian,

concerned.

"No," mumbled Nafiq. "But it doesn't matter. I don't plan on being here that much longer anyway."

"Where are you going?" asked Julian.

"I'm leaving here. I don't want to exist. Why suffer here when I can easily go upstairs?" Nafiq said, emotionless.

"You're talking crazy, and I'm not going to let you do anything to hurt yourself," Julian said.

He could see the intense pain in Nafiq's eyes. He vividly recalls what that type of pain felt like. Two years prior, Julian had voluntarily come out to his mother, certain that she would be receptive and understanding. Instead, she kicked him out onto the streets, forcing him to live in a youth shelter for a few weeks before his aunt (that is, his deceased father's sister) took him in. He considered that experience to be the most traumatic time of his life, and he was determined to help others who faced the same or similar situation.

Julian took out his cellphone. "I'm going to call my aunt right now and see if you can stay with us. She shouldn't have a problem with it."

Nafiq blankly stared in a space, and started to cry again.

Julian held Nafiq. "Everything's going to be all right," he ensured.

✠

Gwendolyn and Reginald sat at the kitchen table, talking on speakerphone with Kiara who was on her cellphone at the Chicago O'Hare airport. She had just arrived in Chicago to attend a fashion expo, which was scheduled to begin the following day.

"Do you know where he is?" asked Kiara.

"No," said Reginald.

"I can't believe you kicked Nafiq out," said Kiara, upset.

"What he's doing is wrong. If he were a drug user or rapist, we wouldn't act any differently," said Gwendolyn.

"Ma, that's absurd. That's not even comparable."

"Despite what you think, it's wrong. I guess, you didn't learn anything from church, either," Gwendolyn said, harshly.

"So you don't care where he is or what he's doing?" asked Kiara.

"Kiara, the point is we won't accept that type of behavior," said Gwendolyn.

"Maybe when he's out in the cold, he'll think about what he's doing, and he'll come to his senses," said Reginald.

"I'm catching the next flight out. I'll see you sometime tomorrow. Bye," Kiara said before hanging up on her parents.

Gwendolyn rolled her eyes, and folded her arms tightly. Reginald frowned and stood up.

"I'll be back," he indicated.

"Where are you going?" asked Gwendolyn.

"I just need some fresh air. I'll be back."

Reginald walked out of the kitchen, grabbed his coat from the hallway closet, and left the house. He got into his car, and drove off into the night. He drove around aimlessly for a half hour, thinking about this new revelation in his family, before he decided to stop at a bar. Reginald hadn't had a drink for nearly twenty years. But his rage, pain, and confusion over Nafiq being gay was so great he yearned for a shot.

Reginald parked his car, and walked into the bar. He ordered whiskey, and sat in the back near the jukebox where a Stylistics song played. He took the shot straight-up, and wondered "Why?" and "How?" He thought he and Gwendolyn had done everything right to raise a strong, straight black man. He reflected and evaluated his relationship with Nafiq. Did he not play enough sports with him as a child? Did he not encourage him enough in life? Wasn't he attentive enough to his son's needs enough growing up? What happened?

Reginald ordered another shot, and swallowed it down. The alcohol hit him hard. He began to reflect on how he had conducted his own life. Was Nafiq paying for the sins of his father? Was Reginald being punished for all the bodies he had left behind in 'Nam, or for the cruel way he had ostracized and disowned his own brother, who was gay? Perhaps, it was genetic.

Reginald ordered a final shot of whiskey, and quickly fell into a drunken depression.

✠

Inside Julian's house, Nafiq and Julian walked upstairs and entered his bedroom.

Julian pointed to one of the two beds in his room, which were adjacent to each other.

"That's your bed," Julian told Nafiq. "Make yourself comfortable."

"Whose bed is it?" asked Nafiq.

"That's my cousin's. He's away at college right now," Julian replied.

Nafiq and Julian sat on their respective beds.

Nafiq lay on his back, and stared at the ceiling; his thoughts distant.

Julian continued to talk. "There are some clothes in that closet, which are also my cousin's. I think you-two may be the same size, so I think they'll fit."

Nafiq cut in. "I can't believe this is happening to me," he said, almost monotone.

"This is something you have to go through. It's hard now. It's hard for everyone at this particular point, but it'll get better. It just takes time to adapt to a new life, so to speak. It's like an emancipation."

"I don't want to adapt to a new life. I preferred the life I had before all of this."

"You preferred lying to everyone about your sexuality and playing mental and emotional games with females? You preferred feeling trapped, uneasy, and hopeless, because you couldn't be who you really were?

"I feel trapped, uneasy, and hopeless now. So, if I had a choice, yes, I would continue living on the DL. At least, that way people wouldn't be judging me and treating me like an outcast, especially my family."

"Nafiq, we live in a judgmental world where people will put you down for anything. Gay, Straight. Black, White. Rich, Poor. Liberal, Conservative. You need to be honest with yourself, and live life the way you want. Ultimately, it doesn't matter what other people think. It matters what you think about yourself. It's about your happiness, no one else's."

"But I'm not happy right now. I'm in this situation because I like dudes. I didn't choose to be this way. I'm being punished for something I have no control over."

Nafiq turned on his side away from Julian, and closed his eyes tightly, trying to hold back his tears. "I shouldn't even be having this conversation. I should be chillin', hangin' out with my bois. Playin' spades or Grand Theft Auto or somethin'. Filling out college applications. Not stressin' about fighting in school, being homeless, and wondering if my family will ever accept me."

"I understand how you feel. I've been through this struggle already, but it will get better. Just be patient."

Suddenly, there was a knock at the door.

"Come in," Julian said.

An attractive, 5'7", mocha-colored woman in her mid-forties entered the room in a nurse's outfit.

"Hey, boy, I just got in," she told Julian.

She looked at Nafiq. "You must be Nafiq."

Nafiq tried to force a smile, but couldn't.

"This is my Aunt Carol," Julian introduced.

"Nice to meet you," said Nafiq, breathily and weak.

"Likewise," Aunt Carol replied.

She continued to talk to Nafiq. "I'm sorry about what happened with your family, but I just wanted to say that you're welcome here, and I want you to make yourself at home. And don't worry, everything will be just fine."

"Thanks," said Nafiq.

"Well, I'm about to take a nice, warm bath and relax. It's been a long, dramatic day at the clinic."

"Why? What happened?" asked Julian.

"This girl's boyfriend found out that she was getting an abortion, and he ended up finding out the clinic's address and bombarding almost every room looking for her. We only have one security guard who's in his fifties, and he was scared to death to confront the guy. So we all had to wait for the cops to come, which took about twenty minutes. And, during that time, the doctors and nurses tried to restrain him and prevent him from hurting his girlfriend."

"That does sound dramatic."

"It was, but I'll leave you-two alone. Have a good night."

"Okay, good night," Julian said.

"Good night," Nafiq told Aunt Carol before she closed the door.

Julian shook his head. "I couldn't work at an abortion clinic."

Nafiq, then, sat up, and faced Julian. "Would you mind if I went to school by myself tomorrow?"

Julian couldn't believe his ears. "Why? You don't want to be seen with me?"

"It's not personal. Like you said, it takes time to adjust. I'm not ready for this yet."

Julian huffed. He couldn't believe Nafiq's audacity. "Sure. If that's what you want to do."

"Thanks for understanding."

Nafiq rolled over on his side. "Good night."

Julian stared at Nafiq with anger in his eyes. "Good night."

Nafiq quickly drifted off to sleep, and immediately found himself in a dream…

He stood outside of his church. The surrounding area was desolate; only the towering brick structure was in view. Nafiq looked around and hesitantly walked into the church. He slowly entered, and suddenly the tall double doors slammed shut. He quickly turned around, forcefully trying to open the doors, but he couldn't. Reverend Douglas stood at his podium, and pointed his finger directly at Nafiq.

"It's not too late, Nafiq," he said. "It's not too late to save yourself from eternal damnation."

Nafiq cringed. He didn't say a word.

Soon thereafter, voices of unseen churchgoers, began to chant "Free yourself. Save yourself. Obey His Word."

Nafiq grabbed his head, closed his eyes, and fell to the

ground, covering his ears, but the chants were still piercing and growing louder. He reopened his eyes, and found himself nailed to the Holy Cross.

Now, his mother stood in front of him with the rest of the family behind her.

"True Hell is separation from God, and that's what you've chosen by participating in this vile lifestyle. You still have a chance to repent, and live a Christian life. To live life like we've raised you to."

Suddenly, the room temperature started to increase. The bodies of the unseen churchgoers suddenly appeared. They swayed back and forth, humming a spiritual.

"This is your last opportunity to avail yourself. The blood of Jesus shall cover you, and set you free. If not…," Gwendolyn lowered her head.

Instantly, blood droplets started to fall upon Nafiq's body from the high, vaulted ceilings, but the droplets, upon contact, evaporated. Nafiq helplessly watched the blood touch his limbs, and then disappear.

Within minutes, Nafiq's body caught on fire, starting with his legs. He frantically tried to break free from the Cross; his body writhing in agony. Burning. Suffocating. But his efforts were futile. Before his body was completely swallowed by the tormenting fire… he woke up, yelling and feeling his skin. He panted heavily, realizing that it was all a dream or, rather, a nightmare. Julian quickly got out of his bed, and walked over to Nafiq. He sat down on the bed, and held Nafiq tightly, rocking him.

"Are you okay?" Julian asked.

Nafiq couldn't speak. He was too distressed. A tear didn't even fall from his eyes.

Julian continued to hold and rock Nafiq as Nafiq stared out of the window into the darkness, shaken up.

"I want to read you something," Julian told Nafiq.

Julian got up from the bed, and walked to his bookshelf. He grabbed the Bible, and walked back to the bed where Nafiq still lay silently.

"I know what'll make you feel better. Just listen."

Julian opened the Bible, and turned to Psalm 69. He started to read.

"I pray to you, Lord, for the time of your favor. God, in your great kindness answer me with your constant help. Rescue me from the mire, do not let me sink. Rescue me from my enemies and from the watery depths…"

CHAPTER 8

Kiara patiently waited in front of the iron gates at Central High in her metallic silver Nissan Altima, hoping to spot Nafiq on his way to school. She waited twenty minutes before she saw her brother walk through the gates by himself. She called out his name. Nafiq looked, and walked up to the car. He got in.

Kiara hugged Nafiq tightly.

"I was so worried about you. Are you all right?" she asked.

"Yeah."

"Mom and Dad told me what happened."

Nafiq frowned up his mouth.

"Why didn't you tell me? All those months of me asking what was wrong with you. You could have confided in me."

Nafiq shrugged his shoulders.

Kiara continued. "You're my little brother. I love you. I would never judge you or do anything to hurt you. You know that."

"No one was supposed to find out. I was trying to prevent going through something like this."

"Where did you stay last night? You weren't on the streets, were you?" asked Kiara.

"No. I stayed with a friend."

Kiara sighed in relief.

"Well, you can stay over my apartment."

"Sis, I'm cool where I am."

"What are you talking about? You need to be with family."

"Kiara, I'm cool. I can handle this."

"But that's not the way it's supposed to be. You'd rather stay over some friend's house instead of coming to stay with your own sister?"

"For right now."

Kiara was shocked and hurt.

"Look, you don't understand."

"Help me understand, then."

"I need to deal with this on my own. It's my own issue. And I don't want to be a burden."

"You're talking nonsense. You wouldn't be a burden. Alonzo and I would love for you to stay with us."

"Kiara, no. I have enough money saved up to survive for a little while, and I'm gonna look for a job today."

"If you want to be stubborn and difficult, fine, but you're always welcome at my house."

"Thanks."

Kiara rolled her eyes. She was extremely upset. Nafiq saw how upset his sister was and partially gave in.

"If you want, I can stay over tonight so we can talk."

"That would be perfect. Alonzo's flying to Atlanta on business today so we'll be able to talk comfortably."

"Cool."

Kiara gave Nafiq a strong, loving hug. "Go ahead to class. I don't want you to be late."

"Aight. See you later on."

Nafiq got out of the car, and walked toward the school's entrance.

Kiara smiled. She was glad to be helping her little brother.

✠

Julian stood at his locker, exchanging books before heading to his next class. Lamar walked up to him.

"Hi, friend," Lamar said, sarcastically.

"Hi," Julian said without looking at Lamar.

"I heard Nafiq is staying with you now," Lamar said.

"Yeah."

"Isn't that lovely? My closest friend steals the only boy I'm interested in. Not only that, you two live together. I guess you'll be getting dicked down every night if you haven't already started."

"First of all, you never expressed that you were into him like that. Secondly, I didn't steal him. I'm just being a friend. Something you consistently fail at."

"I can't believe you. You are so fuckin' shady."

Julian slammed his locker shut.

"And you're fuckin' shallow. Why are you constantly competing with me over men? I'm trying to help him. He has no place to live, and he feels alone. If you're my friend, you should have my back," said Julian.

"Have your back, bitch? I don't think so. Not when you're stabbing me in mine."

"I'm so tired of your bullshit. Save the drama for someone else."

"If you're so tired of my bullshit, cunt, then don't deal with me anymore."

"I won't."

Julian stormed away. Lamar stood at the locker, shocked that Julian didn't attempt to resolve their conflict as he typically did in the past. Julian and Lamar have had feuds before, especially over men, but this time was different. Lamar genuinely felt betrayed by Julian's actions, and Julian was tired of Lamar's "ways." Julian was ready to move on and quash their friendship for good.

✠

Nafiq knocked on the door of Kiara's apartment. A moment later, Alonzo opened the door. Nafiq looked surprised and dismayed.

"What are you doing here?" asked Nafiq.

"Cancelled flight. Sorry to disappoint you with my presence."

Nafiq pushed past Alonzo, and walked into the apartment. He walked into the kitchen where Kiara was taking food out of the stove.

"Wassup?" asked Nafiq.

"Hi. You want me to fix you a plate? I made baked chicken, garlic herb red potatoes, and string beans."

"Not right now."

"Sorry about Alonzo," Kiara whispered to Nafiq.

Alonzo walked into the kitchen, and gave Kiara a sensual kiss on her lips as he stared at Nafiq. Nafiq frowned.

"Alonzo, stop," Kiara said, embarrassed.

Alonzo took Kiara's hand, and started to lead her out of the kitchen. "I have to talk to you," Alonzo told Kiara.

"Can it wait? It's getting late, and I have to talk to Fiq."

He kissed Kiara on the ear. "No, baby. It can't wait. "

"Fiq, excuse me for a few minutes," Kiara said, blushing.

Alonzo led Kiara into the bedroom, and closed the door.

Nafiq sat on the couch, and stared at the bedroom door, angrily. After a couples minutes, sexual moans emanated from the bedroom. Nafiq was appalled. He turned on the television, and turned up the volume to drown the moans, but they got louder. He lay back, and closed his eyes, frowning.

✠

About an hour later, Kiara walked into the living room in her nightgown, and noticed pillows burying Nafiq's head.

"Fiq, are you awake?" whispered Kiara.

He didn't respond. He was fast asleep. She frowned, and walked back into the bedroom, closing the door behind herself. She got into the bed next to Alonzo who was just laying there. Alonzo turned over, facing Kiara. He started caressing her inner thigh and sensuously kissing her breasts.

"You ready for round two?" he asked her in between kisses.

Kiara moved away slightly. "Stop, Alonzo."

He started to softly tweak her nipples.

"Alonzo, no!" she said, strongly.

Alonzo stopped, and slammed his head on the pillow next to her, facing the ceiling.

"What's wrong?" he asked.

"I was thinking about Nafiq. He doesn't have anywhere permanent to stay, and I want him to live here."

"What?" Alonzo quickly blurted. He sat up.

"Is there something wrong with that?" Kiara asked.

"Yeah, I don't think that's a good idea," Alonzo said in a strong, disapproving tone. "If you forgot, I'm supposed to be leaving my place to move in with you next week."

"You are so selfish sometimes," said Kiara.

"There's only one bedroom here. Where would he sleep?"

"On the couch. He can only stay at a friend's house for so long, and I don't foresee my parents letting him come back right now. We're his only other option."

"Okay. Let's say he lives here for a week or two, but after that time, your parents still don't want him to come back home. Then, what?"

"He'll continue to live with us. I'm not going to abandon him."

"Kiara, we're our own family. He dug this hole for himself."

"I can't believe you!"

"Baby, I'm willing to help, but I'm opposed to him living with us."

"Why? Is it because he's gay? I know you don't like gay people. You've expressed that many times, but he's family. He's my brother. And I'm not going to turn my back on him."

"I'm your man. You're not just going to allow him to live with us without my permission."

Kiara looked at Alonzo like he had lost his mind. She got out of the bed, and grabbed her pillows and sheets.

"I don't know what you're on, but I'm going to let you sleep on it."

Kiara walked out of the bedroom, slamming the door behind her.

Alonzo gritted his teeth.

✠

Gwendolyn sat in front of the television, viewing old VHS home videos of the family. Her eyes were bloodshot.

On the television screen, a four-year old Nafiq tried to make baskets in his miniature basketball hoop. Reginald lifted Nafiq up so he could make a dunk. Then, a little girl ran up, same age as Nafiq, and gave him a kiss on his cheek.

Tears rolled from Gwendolyn's eyes.

Reginald walked into the room, and sat next to Gwendolyn, holding her hand and embracing her. Gwendolyn rested her head on Reginald's shoulder. They stared at the screen blankly.

CHAPTER 9

Michael Baisden's "Love, Lust and Lies" show blared on the radio as Nafiq waited in the living room for Kiara to finish getting dressed. She rushed into the living room.

"Let's go," Kiara said, heading towards the front door.

Nafiq followed, and they left the apartment.

In the car, Kiara started the ignition, put the car into gear, and headed for the freeway.

"Did you sleep well?" Kiara asked.

"I slept okay."

"I apologize about last night. I promise I'll make it up to you."

Nafiq didn't respond.

Kiara looked at Nafiq to read his expression. He appeared unhappy.

"How about I take you to dinner at your favorite Jamaican spot tonight?" suggested Kiara.

"Naw. I already have plans."

Kiara looked disappointed.

Nafiq stared out of the side window, and noticed a bulletin board sign, indicating the number of African-American women in the United States who have been infected with HIV to date. He cringed. Kiara noticed the sign as well.

"Isn't that awful?" asked Kiara.

"What?"

"All those black females infected with HIV. It just seems unreal. You'd think they would have asked about their man's sexual history or, at least, protected themselves."

"Are you using protection with Alonzo?" Nafiq asked.

"What kind of question is that?" asked Kiara.

"An important one since we're on the subject," said Nafiq.

Nafiq continued to stare out of the window. He waited for a response, and dreaded what Kiara's answer may be.

Kiara looked at him. "No, we're not."

Nafiq whipped his head around, and faced Kiara. "What!" he shouted in shock.

"What's the matter?"

"You just saw the billboard sign. And didn't you just comment about women asking their men about their sexual history and about protecting themselves?"

"I was talking about females who have casual sex. My situation is different. Alonzo and I are in a monogamous relationship, we're engaged, and we're trying to have a baby."

Nafiq frowned. He couldn't believe his ears. "You're trying to have a baby?"

"Yes. We're both ready to start raising a family together."

"Aren't you moving too fast? Do you even know for sure what Alonzo is really like?"

"Nafiq, come on. We've been together for four years. I know everything I need to know about him. He's going to be a fantastic husband and father."

Kiara sighed. "I knew you didn't like him."

"Kiara, this has nothing to do with me liking Alonzo."

"What does it have to do with, then?"

Nafiq took a deep breath. "There's something you need to know about your fiancée."

"Okay. What is it?"

Nafiq took another deep breath. "I don't know how to explain."

"Take your time."

Nafiq lowered his head. "He's cheating on you."

Kiara looked stunned.

Nafiq quickly grabbed the door rest. He looked at the speedometer. It quickly hit 75 mph.

"Kiara, slow down."

"I know you're going through a lot right now and you may not like Alonzo, but how can you make up something awful like that? Why are you trying to hurt me?"

"Sis, I'm not trying to hurt you. I'm for real."

Tears began to fill Kiara's eyes. The car accelerated, again. The speedometer hit 105 mph. Kiara weaved in and out of lanes and between cars on the icy roads. A look of horror overtook Nafiq's face.

"Kiara, please slow down before you kill us."

"How do you know he's cheating?" asked Kiara.

"I caught him having sex."

"Caught him having sex? With who? Where?"

"He was doing it to some guy in the restroom at the mall."

"A guy in the mall restroom?"

Pain quickly consumed Kiara's face.

"And when did all this take place?" she asked.

"A week or so ago. I didn't know how to tell you. I'm sorry."

Kiara abruptly stopped the car. They were now outside of Central High. She looked at Nafiq, disappointed.

"Kiara, please don't be upset with me. It was difficult trying to tell you."

Kiara didn't respond.

Nafiq got out of the car, and closed the door.

Kiara sped off. She decided to drive back to her apartment. She was too crazed and upset to go to work. Her conversation with Nafiq continued to echo in her mind. She always felt that Nafiq didn't like Alonzo, but it was hard to believe that he would make something so horrible up about Alonzo. Nevertheless, Nafiq's words weren't enough proof.

She had to find out the truth on her own.

After a ten minute drive, Kiara parked her car, and walked up the stairs to her apartment. She entered, took off her coat, and sat on the sofa. She picked up the *Yellow Pages*, and started panning through it. She was undeniably angry, horrified, and distraught. She stopped on one of the pages, and dialed a number on her phone. She waited for someone to pick up.

"Good afternoon, RJM Investigators. How may I help you?" a male voice answered.

Kiara sat on the sofa with the receiver to her head, trying to find the strength to speak.

✠

Julian sat on his bed, cornrowing Nafiq's hair. Nafiq sat on the floor between Julian's legs. Nafiq shook his head.

"I should have never told my sister about her fiancée."

"Come on now. We've been through this a thousand times today. You did the right thing. It's better she found out now instead of 5, 10, 20 years down the road. She has a right to know that her man lives a dual life."

"But me telling her hasn't benefited anyone. I don't even think she believes me. She probably despises me now."

"I highly doubt it. She's just in shock and very hurt. Not at you, just at the entire situation and at her man."

"I guess."

"Maybe you should stay with her," suggested Julian.

Nafiq smiled. "You're trying to get rid of me now?"

"No, but you and your sister need each other. You're both going through a hard time right now, and you two can help each other out."

Nafiq nodded. "True."

"And, at least, you have the option to stay with a relative and to talk with them. I didn't have anyone for awhile."

Nafiq turned, and faced Julian. "Well, I appreciate everything you've done for me. If it wasn't for you, I don't know what I would have done."

Julian smiled. "That's what friends are for."

Nafiq turned away from Julian. "I also apologize for wanting to go to school without you. That was insensitive and inconsiderate."

"No problem."

Julian reached for the hair gel, and accidentally bumped the cut above Nafiq's eyebrow with the metal comb.

Nafiq flinched. "Yo, be careful."

Julian leaned down, and softly kissed the healing cut.

Nafiq turned around and looked at Julian, shocked that Julian had just kissed him. Julian didn't know how to interpret Nafiq's expression, so he apologized.

Nafiq smiled. "You know, you're the first guy to ever kiss me."

Julian returned the smile. "I don't think an eyebrow really counts."

Nafiq reached, and pulled Julian's head toward him, giving him a long, wet, passionate kiss.

"Now, does that count?"

Julian tried to catch his breath. "Umm..., that definitely counts," Julian said, grinning and blushing.

Nafiq got on his knees, and was face to face with Julian. He gazed into Julian's gleaming eyes, and wrapped his arms around him, moving Julian closer to his body. Nafiq pushed his tongue into Julian's mouth, and kissed Julian hungrily. Julian squeezed Nafiq, and kissed him with the same amount of passion. Nafiq, then, began to work his way to Julian's neck and ear lobe. Julian closed his eyes, and breathed deeply. Savoring. Anticipating.

Nafiq stood up from the floor, and took off his shirt, revealing his muscular physique and six-pack. Julian moved in closer, and licked around Nafiq's navel as he massaged his crotch.

Julian felt Nafiq's manhood swell through his jeans.

"Damn, boy. You see what you doin' to me," Nafiq said.

Julian gripped Nafiq's pole harder as he nibbled on it through the jeans.

Nafiq moaned, and gently pushed Julian on his back.

He slowly unbuttoned Julian's shirt, and began to kiss and caress Julian's chest. He flicked Julian's nipples with his tongue, and started to suck on them. Julian's body shuddered. He moaned in ecstacy.

"Ahh..."

Nafiq kissed Julian on his eyebrow, and looked into his sparkling eyes. "I wanna feel you. I wanna be inside you."

"Are you sure?" Julian asked.

"Yeah. I'm real sure," Nafiq said, his concrete piece trying to break through his jeans.

Julian kissed Nafiq on the lips. "Okay."

Nafiq lifted his body, and took off his jeans and boxers, exposing his long, thick stem. Julian looked at it, his mouth watering, his body yearning to feel it. He ran his mouth up and down Nafiq's shaft, and teased the head with his tongue. He, then, deep-throated it, devouring it, feeling Nafiq's pulsating sensation.

"Ahh, shit," Nafiq yelled out as a wave of pleasure shot across his body.

Julian stopped, and removed his shirt, jeans and briefs.

"It's that time," Julian said as he kissed Nafiq on the lips. He reached for his wallet on the nightstand, and pulled out a condom.

Nafiq anxiously took the condom from Julian, and immediately slipped it on.

"Lay on your back," Julian instructed.

Nafiq lay on his back, and Julian straddled him.

They made love for hours- kissing, licking, groping, sucking, caressing, riding, and grinding. Afterwards, they cuddled, and fell asleep in each other's arms.

CHAPTER 10

Simone stood at her locker, exchanging books. Nafiq walked up to her. She turned around, and greeted him.

"What's up, stranger?" Simone said, ecstatic.

"What's good?" asked Nafiq.

"Everything's good. I've been wanting to talk to you about the party. I'm really looking forward to going with you. We're gonna have a wonderful time."

Nafiq swallowed hard. "I actually need to talk to you about the party."

Simone looked concerned. "Is everything all right?"

"Yeah, but I won't be able to go."

"Why?" Simone asked.

"It's complicated."

"Is it something I did?" asked Simone.

"Not at all."

"Then, what?"

"You're a very beautiful and intelligent girl. I just don't want to lead you on."

Simone became extremely saddened.

"So you're saying you've been playing with my emotions this entire time, and you were never interested in me?"

"I like you, but-"

Simone slammed her locker shut. "Don't speak, Nafiq. I guess, the rumors are true."

Simone rolled her eyes, and walked away.

Nafiq leaned up against the locker, upset that he had hurt Simone but even more devastated that rumors about his sexuality were now a hot topic among his peers.

Nafiq slung his book bag over his shoulder, and headed to his fourth period class. As he walked through the hallway, his fellow classmates stared at him, and whispered among themselves. Nafiq felt uncomfortable. He knew they were talking about him, spreading poisonous rumors. Defaming him. But he was determined to not let it bother him. He was going to shake it off as best as he could.

Before entering his History class, his cellphone rang. He checked the caller ID, and saw that it was Kiara. He answered.

"Wassup, sis?"

"Do you have practice today?"

"Yeah. Why?"

"I'm going to pick you up afterwards," said Kiara.

"Why?"

"I spoke to Mom and Dad, and convinced them to have a family meeting tonight."

"Aight."

"So what time does your practice end?"

"6:30."

"Okay. I'll meet you outside the gym at 7:00."

"Cool. See you, then."

"Okay, bye."

Kiara and Nafiq hung up their phones. Nafiq stood for a moment and pondered. Were his parents finally coming around?

Nafiq faintly smiled, and walked into the classroom.

✠

Kiara and Nafiq pulled up in front of the Johnson residence. They stepped out into the cold air, and tracked through the deep snow toward the front door.

"You nervous?" Kiara asked.

"Yeah. I just hope everything works out."

Kiara rang the doorbell. Gwendolyn opened the door, and looked at Nafiq and Kiara icily. She walked back into the living room without greeting them. Kiara and Nafiq looked at each other, and walked into the house. They took off their coats, hung them in the hallway closet, and walked into the living room. They sat down.

"Reggie. Marcus. Please come in here," Gwendolyn informed.

Reginald and Marcus entered the living room.

Reginald looked at Nafiq, and frowned. Marcus looked at Nafiq, disappointedly. They took a seat.

"As you know, we're here to have a family meeting. We need to get everything out in the open, and discuss everyone's feelings," said Kiara.

Gwendolyn immediately jumped in. "What that boy is feeling is wrong."

"Mom, we agreed to have a civil discussion. Please calm down."

"I can't have a civil discussion about this. Homosexuality is unnatural and ungodly. Nafiq can be delivered from this. He just needs to believe in His Word."

"I believe and my faith won't change, but this is who I am. This is what I am. I didn't make this choice. I've always been this way."

"This isn't who you are. This isn't the way we raised you to be. We raised a strong, proud, respectable black man, and a devout Christian," said Reginald.

"And somehow, you've strayed. You need to wake up and acknowledge that there's only one way, and that's God's way. I don't wish to associate myself with anyone who believes or acts to the contrary," Gwendolyn added.

"So you're just going to ostracize your son forever? He just said that he didn't choose this lifestyle. Why can't you try to just understand?" pleaded Kiara.

"That's an excuse. Nothing will ever justify this behavior. Nothing!" Reginald exclaimed.

"Dad, you're being unreasonable and unfair," said Kiara.

"I'll tell you what's unfair, Kiara. Me having a sissy punk as a son," said Reginald. "I now have to go to the shop everyday and live in this community with people snickering and talking behind my back, because my son is gay. Do you know how disgraceful that is? To me? To this family?"

Nafiq quickly stood up, angry and upset by his father's words.

"Just because I'm attracted to men doesn't make me a sissy punk. I'm not any less of a man or human being, either. I still have feelings. I still have goals and aspirations. And I still have love for my family no matter what is said or done. And if you can't accept me for me, then that's your loss."

"Well, we won't accept you. Not in this household, not in our lives," said Gwendolyn. "You've given up on the Lord. Your soul is lost."

"You have no right to judge me. My salvation and relationship with God is only between me and God. His love is unconditional and all-inclusive. If you were true Christians, like you always claim, then you would know that and wouldn't judge me. You would leave the situation in God's hands."

"Don't you dare turn this around," snapped Gwendolyn.

"If you want to disown me forever, cool. But in the end, you'll be hurting yourselves more than me. Your attacks on me say a lot more about you and your spirit than me."

"Get out of my house," growled Reginald.

Nafiq walked out the room. Kiara stood up, saddened.

"You shouldn't be defending him, Kiara," said Gwendolyn. "You're no better than him."

Kiara walked out of the room, and went to the car.

Gwendolyn and Reginald looked at each other even more upset than before.

Marcus got up, and rushed after Nafiq.

Outside, Marcus called for Nafiq who was walking to the car with Kiara.

Nafiq turned around, and walked up to his brother.

"Why are you doing this?" asked Marcus.

"Doing what? What am I doing, Marcus?" Nafiq asked, angry.

"You're hurting the family, and you can fix it. You can change."

"I can't change."

"Well, what the Hell happened, man? Did you mess around with some guy, and now you think you're gay?"

"No, I didn't. I've always been gay."

"How? There aren't any other family members who are gay so it's not genetic. You grew up with a mother and a father who are still happily married so it's not sociological. You don't hang around white folks so you couldn't have picked up any of their traits. So, what? I want to know," demanded Marcus.

Nafiq frowned. "To be such an intelligent, educated, Ivy-League brotha, you are so ignorant. But I wouldn't expect you to understand, anyway."

"Well, I guess not. But I agree with Mom and Dad. I

don't respect or accept this lifestyle you've chosen. It's evil, plain and simple. And as long as you like banging other guys or whatever you do, then you're not my brother. I don't know you."

"Cool. And I don't know you, either,"

Nafiq walked away, trying to hold back his tears. He got into the car, and closed the door. Kiara was in the driver's seat, waiting for him.

"What did Marcus say?" Kiara asked.

Nafiq shook his head, reclined his seat, and closed his eyes, trying to hold it all in.

☒

In his car, Alonzo drove through the streets of Southwest Philly. Behind him, Investigator Raul Martinez, the private eye Kiara hired to present tangible evidence of Alonzo's infidelity, drove in his car.

After unknowingly being followed for twenty minutes, Alonzo finally pulled in front of a residence and parked. He got out of the car, cautiously looked around, and walked onto the porch of a brick rowhouse. He rang the doorbell.

Martinez sat in his car across the street, watching.

A brown-skinned brotha in a white tank top and grey athletic shorts came to the door, and looked out the peephole.

"Code?" he asked.

"12 inches," Alonzo whispered.

The man opened the door, and let Alonzo into the dimly

lit house. They shook hands.

"Donation is fifteen," the man said.

Alonzo reached into his pocket, took out fifteen dollars, and handed it to the man.

"If you walk straight ahead, there's a room on your left. The guy in there will do your clothes check. Also, there's plenty of lube and alcohol. If you wanna smoke some weed, there's a room for that upstairs."

Alonzo nodded.

"Enjoy yourself."

Alonzo nodded, again, and proceeded to the clothes check room.

Outside, Martinez continued to watch the scene. Within a ten minute period, he had witnessed eight men enter the residence. Now, a short, stocky fella walked onto the porch. Martinez quickly got out of the car, and hurried across the street.

Martinez walked up behind the short, stocky fella, and he greeted Martinez by nodding his head. Martinez nodded back.

The fella rang the doorbell, and waited for a response. The same doorman looked out the peephole.

"Code?"

"12 inches," the fella whispered.

The doorman opened the door, and let the fella and Martinez in. He collected their donation, and instructed them where to put their clothes.

Uncomfortable, Martinez walked to the clothes check room. He waited for the fella to undress and leave before taking off his own clothes. Martinez left his boxers on, and put on a pair of covert eyeglasses, which contained a video module the size of a grain of rice. The video module, which was hidden in the frame of the eyeglasses, functioned as a mini video camera, and transferred all of the visual information to Martinez's portable laptop computer.

Martinez walked around the house, observing. The rooms in the house were lit with blue and red neon lights. The entire house smelled of sweat, sex, alcohol, weed, and more sex. 50 Cent played in the background. All types of brothas roamed the house. Some completely nude. Others only wearing boxers and/or tank tops.

Martinez looked in one of the rooms, and witnessed a wild, male orgy. He continued to walk around, and peeked into the kitchen where he noticed a man having his ass eaten out on the kitchen table. Martinez held his stomach, trying to prevent himself from regurgitating. He continued to roam the house, and walked upstairs, looking for Alonzo.

Martinez glanced into what appeared to be the master bedroom, and saw Alonzo with six other guys, sucking and fucking. Alonzo lay on his back as one of the men sucked Alonzo and got screwed at the same time. Martinez stood in the doorway, watching and letting the video iris capture all of the action.

One of the men motioned for Martinez to join in. Martinez shook his head, and continued to stand at the bedroom entrance, recording Alonzo and his sexual escapade.

Martinez was shocked at was taking place. How could a

man do this to his girlfriend or wife? Hell! How could he do this at all? Having sex with another man was trifling and disgusting. "Maricones. Escoria," he thought to himself.

As Martinez captured the action, a young boi walked passed, and casually grabbed Martinez's crotch through his boxers.

"Ay, Papi! You got a big dick," the young boi said.

Martinez forcefully moved the boi's hand away. "Don't touch me again."

Shocked by Martinez's response, the young boi quickly averted his eyes, and quietly walked away.

Now angry, Martinez decided that enough footage had been captured, and decided to leave the house. He walked back downstairs, got dressed, and left. He got into his car, locked the doors, and took out his cellphone. He dialed Kiara's number.

"Hello," Kiara answered.

"Ms. Johnson, this is Mr. Martinez. Let's meet tomorrow morning around 9 a.m. I have some information for you."

"Okay," said Kiara, trying to hold back her tears. She hung up the phone, and took a seat on the sofa chair across from Nafiq.

Nafiq looked at Kiara, and noticed she had suddenly become bothered.

"Sis, who was that? Is everything all right?" Nafiq asked, concerned.

"Wrong number," she replied.

Kiara picked up the remote control, and started skimming

through the cable channels in a daze.

✠

Gwendolyn lay in bed, thinking and staring at Nafiq's basketball picture on the wall, deeply bothered by tonight's confrontation with Nafiq and Kiara. Next to Gwendolyn lay Reginald, who was attempting to read the Business section of *The New York Times*, but couldn't. He was too distraught over his own guilt and pain for believing that he was to blame for Nafiq's homosexuality.

Gwendolyn broke the stark silence. "Reggie, do you think it's all my fault?"

Reginald put down his newspaper, but didn't face Gwendolyn.

"Is what all your fault?" he asked, annoyed.

"The reason Nafiq is the way he is."

"Why would you think something like that? Why would you be the reason?" he asked, his tone becoming hostile.

"I'm just trying to figure out why," said Gwendolyn. "Do you think something happened to him as a child? Do you think that one of the babysitters may have touched him?"

Reginald finally faced Gwendolyn.

"If Nafiq was molested, then he or Kiara would have said something by now. Point is, we are not to blame. We did everything in our power to raise our children properly."

"Maybe it's just a phase."

"Gwen, please. Let's just drop it, and go to bed. I'm

tired."

Reginald placed the newspaper on the nightstand, and turned on his side away from Gwendolyn. He turned out the light.

"Good night," Reginald said, closing his eyes.

Gwendolyn got out of the bed, and left the room.

Gwendolyn walked to the bathroom, closed the door, and took off her slippers and nightgown. She sat on the edge of the tub, naked, and started running the bath water, adjusting the cold and hot temperature to make it soothing. She watched the tub fill, watching the ebb and flow of the rushing water, listening to the sharp, splashing sounds. Once the bathtub filled up, she climbed in, and sunk into the water. She leaned back and closed her eyes, letting the water come up to her neck. She was deeply troubled. She couldn't help but to wonder if she was the cause for Nafiq's homosexuality. For days, she reflected on her life, and she had come to her own realization- she was the reason Nafiq was gay. It is her sins her son was paying for.

Tears trickled down her cheeks as she tried to cope. She had tried for many years to keep this particular sin a secret, but it was now haunting her every thought. She reflected back to when Reginald had gone to Georgia to help his ailing mother. At that time, she and Reginald were having marital problems, and she felt that a divorce was imminent. Distraught and in need of comfort, she began having an illicit affair with one of the senior associates at her law firm- Mr. Charles Harris, Esq. Reginald had not even been in Georgia for a month when the affair commenced. After a few weeks of loving Mr. Harris in the office, in the file room, and in his condo, she learned that she was pregnant with her third child- Nafiq. She immediately stopped the affair and prayed for God to forgive her. She didn't mean to be an adulterer. She was just caught up in the emotion. And now she had to revisit this secret, and believe that He didn't forgive her. Maybe He was punishing her for never telling Reginald, for never telling anyone.

Suddenly, a shooting pain ran up her left side, and she quickly opened her eyes, holding on to herself. She started to softly rub her side.

The water was cold, and she was ready to get out of the tub. But before she did, she put her hands together in prayer, and asked once again to be forgiven. And, then, maybe Nafiq would be washed of his sin, too.

CHAPTER 11

Kiara sat in her car outside of her apartment, waiting to meet with Investigator Martinez. Although she knew he was going to produce incriminating evidence, based on the tone of their conversation the previous day, she was still extremely nervous and upset. She tried to sip on some green tea to calm her nervous, but she couldn't drink it. She felt knots in her stomach and throat.

After a fifteen minute wait, Investigator Martinez walked up to the car, carrying a jet black portfolio. Kiara unlocked the door, and Martinez got into the car.

"Hi, Ms. Johnson."

"Hi," said Kiara, weakly.

He handed the portfolio to Kiara, and she opened it, slowly taking the pictures out, one by one. Clearly, it was Alonzo at a sex party with various men, engaging in group sex, drinking, doing lines of cocaine, and having more uninhibited sex.

Kiara abruptly threw the pictures down, and broke down, crying.

Martinez rubbed Kiara's shoulder, but she moved her shoulder away, not wanting to be touched.

Kiara continued to cry, hiding her face with her hands. The flood of tears ran through her fingers, along her hands. She was devastated. Humiliated. Angry. She thought she had found the man of her dreams. Educated. Intelligent. Successful. Ambitious. Handsome. Monogamous. But her ace of a man, whom she loved deeply, whom she sometimes loved more than herself, had failed to be truthful about a major part of his life. The unbearable pain penetrated her soul, puncturing her spirit.

"I'm sorry," Martinez said.

"No, I'm the sorry one," Kiara replied. "I can't believe I didn't see this in him. How could I be so blind?"

✠

Inside of the building that housed Triple P Records' offices, Alonzo sat at his desk, negotiating on the phone with an artist's manager.

Suddenly, Kiara burst through Alonzo's office door,

carrying the jet black portfolio. Alonzo's receptionist ran behind Kiara.

"Mr. Miller, I've called security. This crazy woman is claiming she's your fiancée."

"I'll call you back," Alonzo told the manager. He hung up the phone, and stood up.

"Danielle, she is my fiancée."

Danielle's jaw dropped. "I'm so sorry, Mr. Miller. I didn't know."

"It's okay. Just let security know everything's all right."

"Okay."

Danielle looked at Kiara. "I deeply apologize. Mr. Miller never mentioned he had a fiancée."

Kiara looked at the receptionist with a cold stare.

The receptionist left the office, closing the door behind herself.

Alonzo walked over to give Kiara a hug, but she moved back.

"Baby, don't be upset about that. She's my new receptionist. She didn't know I was engaged."

"I'm not angry about that."

"Then, what's wrong?"

Alonzo reached for Kiara's hand, but she moved her hand away.

"I want you to listen to what I have to say, and I want you to tell me the truth."

"Sure."

"During the four years we've been together, have you

ever been with anyone else?"

"No, not at all."

"Absolutely, no one?" asked Kiara.

"No, no one. I love you. I want to spend the rest of my life with you. I haven't been with any other females since we've been together."

"Have you ever been with any men?"

Alonzo was stunned by the question.

"Have I ever been with any men? Hell, no! Why would you ask me something like that?"

"It's a valid question."

"A valid question? I'm not a faggot. How dare you suggest that? Where's this coming from?"

"You're a damn liar," yelled Kiara.

"What the Hell am I lying about?"

"You're sleeping with men. Just admit it."

"That shit is abnormal and disgusting. I never touched another man in my life, and I never plan to."

Kiara took out the photos from the portfolio, and threw them at Alonzo. They scattered across the floor. He picked one of the photos up, recognizing himself in the photo. He was topping some guy over the shoulder style while other men were in the background watching and doing their thing, too.

Alonzo tried to remain calm.

"What's this?"

"You know what it is. It's you fucking some guy at some trifling sex party."

"Kiara, this isn't me. These photos aren't authentic."

"What's not authentic about them? That's your face, your hands, and your dick in some guy's ass, obviously enjoying what you're doing."

"Baby, it's not me," said Alonzo, calmly. "I swear. You know this industry is a snake pit. Someone's trying to destroy my career and our relationship."

"You don't have to act or pretend for me anymore. I know the truth. I just wish you would have had the decency and respect for me to at least protect yourself when messing around with these people."

Kiara slid her engagement ring off of her finger, and threw it at him. He caught it.

"I hope it's not too late to renew your lease, 'cause you're getting out of my apartment and my life."

Alonzo forcefully grabbed Kiara's wrist. "You are my fiancée. You will not leave me. I love you."

Kiara broke free from his grasp. "Don't you ever touch me like that again or it will be the last time you touch anyone," Kiara threatened.

"I'm sorry, baby. I'm just a little angry. Let's talk this out."

Kiara rolled her eyes, and left the office, slamming the door behind her.

Alonzo's face tightened. He punched the wall. "Fuck!"

✠

In her bedroom, Kiara folded her clothes while Nafiq finished ironing one of his shirts. "Where are you two going?"

asked Kiara.

"Julian wants to go to dinner and see an exhibition at the art museum."

Kiara smiled. "That sounds pleasant. You have an intellectual and cultured man on your hands."

"I know I do."

"But that's good. I'm happy for you."

"Thanks."

Suddenly, the doorbell buzzed.

"I'll get it," Nafiq said.

He walked into the living room, and looked through the peephole.

"Yes? May I help you?" asked Nafiq.

Standing outside the door was a short, skinny white man delivering flowers.

"I have three dozen roses for Ms. Kiara Johnson," the flower man said.

"That's my sister," Nafiq said as he opened up the door. "I'll take them," he told the delivery man, signing for the delivery.

The man handed Nafiq the flowers, and he closed the door.

Nafiq walked into the living room, and placed them onto the table. He opened the attached card, which read: *Kiara, I love you. Don't let our love go. Love, Zo.*

Nafiq frowned.

Kiara walked into the living room, and saw the flowers.

"Are they from Alonzo?" asked Kiara.

"Yeah."

Kiara quickly snatched them from the table, and threw them into the trash.

"He's been calling my cellphone and emailing me all day, apologizing. I just wish he'd stop."

Suddenly, Kiara started to waver back and forth. She took a seat on the sofa, and held her head with her hands.

"Are you all right?" asked Nafiq, taking a seat next to her.

"I'm just a little nauseous and dizzy. I think it's the Chinese food I had earlier. I'm just going to lay down. I've had a long day."

"I think I should stay here with you. You don't look well."

"Nafiq, I'm fine," Kiara insisted. "There's no need to postpone your date. Go ahead and enjoy yourself."

"You're sure?"

"I'm sure. Go on, boy."

"Aight. I hope you feel better, sis. If you need anything while I'm out, please give me a call."

"Thanks. I will if I need to."

Nafiq gave Kiara a loving hug. He put on his shirt and left the bedroom to get his coat. Kiara walked into her bathroom, and turned on the sink faucet. She leaned in and splashed cold water on her face. She sighed deeply and lifted her head. She looked at her reflection in the mirror, and what she saw was a frightened young woman. She turned off the sink faucet, dried her face off, and left the bathroom. In her bedroom, she got under the sheets, and turned onto her side. She tightly clutched the soft, silk covers on her bed, crying hysterically. Mascara ran down her cheeks, staining the sheets.

✠

Nafiq opened up the door for Julian, and they walked into Carlucci's Italian Restaurant. They were immediately greeted by the male host and were asked to wait to be seated. Julian looked around the restaurant and was very impressed. The restaurant had a chic, contemporary décor, full of rich beiges and yellows. In the middle of the restaurant, a beautiful brick fireplace roared.

A petite, white female walked up to Nafiq and Julian.

"Please follow me, gentlemen," she politely instructed as she showed them to their table near the fireplace.

They sat down, and got comfortable.

"I'll come back shortly," the waitress said.

Julian smiled. "This is such a nice restaurant. Have you been here before?"

"Yeah. My family sometimes comes here on special occasions."

Julian blushed. Nafiq smiled.

They picked up their menus, and checked out the many selections, all written in Italian with English translations.

"Everything on here sounds so delicious. I don't know if I'll be able to decide."

The waitress returned to the table.

"Good evening, gentlemen. Welcome to Carlucci's. My

name is Becky, and I'll be your waitress for tonight. Would you like an appetizer to start out with?" the waitress inquired.

Nafiq looked at Julian. "You see anything you like?"

"The three cheese foccacia bread with fresh, herb tomato sauce sounds good."

"We'll get one order of the foccacia," Nafiq said, "and I would also like a Coke."

"I'll take a ginger ale," Julian added.

"Okay, I'll place your order, and be right back."

"Thanks," Nafiq said.

The waitress walked away.

Julian grinned.

"What's on your mind?" asked Nafiq.

"I was just recalling the first time I saw you. I was with Lamar, and he was checking you out through the gym windows at school. I remember telling him 'You better be careful. You know how those DL boys are.' I was completely opposed to him talking to you, because I thought you were nothing but trouble. I was wrong, though, and I'm just thankful that we had a chance to connect."

"Me, too. To be honest, I was trying to avoid you and Lamar, but, if you hadn't put that smile on me in the club, we probably wouldn't be here right now."

"Hey, I know my smile can hook a brotha."

"I'm sure you do," Nafiq smiled.

The waitress returned, and placed their drinks and appetizer on the table.

"Have you two decided on an entree?"

Nafiq nodded for Julian to order first.

"I'll have the penne di pesce."

"And I'll have the pollo scarpariello," Nafiq said.

"Okay," the waitress said as she took the menus.

Nafiq and Julian took a sip of their drinks.

"Have you spoken to Lamar since your argument?" Nafiq asked.

"No. I think it's best I cut him loose. For years, he's always been in competition with me, and has done some real shady things to me. I've always been a good friend to him. I tried to accept him for who he is, but there's only so much a person can take."

"I feel you. I haven't talked to my bois since our fight in the cafeteria. It's real messed up how someone you've been friends with for so long just turns on you. Me and Shawn had been friends since elementary school. We were tight."

Nafiq frowned, still upset about his loss of friendship with Shawn.

"Believe me, I understand," Julian replied.

Nafiq broke off a piece of the foccacia bread, and dipped it into the sauce.

"I have a question," Julian asserted.

"Shoot."

"Where do you want to go to school once you graduate?"

"Duke. They have one of the best college basketball teams, and it's a great school academically."

"What about after college?"

"I want to continue the family legacy, and start my own

business. I plan to run my own sports management company. I'll most likely major in Business at Duke, and then go to grad school and get my M.B.A. That is, if I don't make it into the pros. What about you? Are you going to stay in Philly? You look like a UPenn man."

"No. I want to go to NYU, and study political science. Then, I'm going to law school. I see myself as a civil rights attorney."

"That's what's up."

Julian began twirling his glass around, nervously.

"I have another question," Julian said.

"Talk to me?"

"If you were in a relationship with someone, and they ended up living far away from you, would you still want to be in a relationship with that person?"

"Wow. That's a big question. I guess, if I was really feelin' that person, I wouldn't mind being in a long distance relationship."

Julian took a sip of his soda.

"If that happens to us, is that what you would want to do?" asked Nafiq.

"Are we actually in a relationship?"

"If you don't consider us to be in one, right now, I would like to be," Nafiq said.

Julian smiled brightly. His faced looked as if the Heavens opened up.

"I would love that," Julian responded.

Nafiq smiled.

The waitress returned, and placed Julian and Nafiq's food in front of them, and they started eating.

Julian smiled. "I'm really having a good time."

"Me, too."

Nafiq, then, lifted his glass. "To a great dinner with my sexy, baby boi."

Julian lifted his glass. "To a great dinner with my man."

They clacked their glasses, and continued to eat, talk, and engulf themselves in each other's presence.

CHAPTER 12

In the high school gymnasium, the basketball team scrimmaged each other. Throughout the practice, Nafiq was fierce and focused. His game had definitely improved.

Toward the end of the scrimmage, Nafiq dribbled toward the hoop, driving in to make a slam dunk. As he soared through the air, one of his teammates quickly ran up and submarined him, knocking his legs off balance and causing him to flip backwards. Nafiq crashed to the ground headfirst. He lay motionless. His eyes stared at the ceiling, not moving.

"That's what happens when you have faggots on the court. That's for my cousin, Simone, too," the teammate whispered to Nafiq.

Coach Franklin and the other teammates ran over to Nafiq.

Brian, one of Nafiq's teammates, shoved the culprit out of the way. "What the fuck you do that for?" he yelled, angrily.

Coach Franklin kneeled down next to Nafiq. "Nafiq, are you okay?"

Nafiq didn't respond. He was unconscious.

"Someone call the ambulance now!" Coach Franklin shouted.

✠

The dreary fluorescent lights created a cold, grayish cast inside the room. Kiara lay on the hard clinic bed in a baby blue hospital gown.

Dr. Burns, a forty-something looking white man, handed a document to his nurse who happened to be Julian's aunt, Carol.

"Can you make a copy of the consent form?" Dr. Burns asked.

Nurse Carol nodded, and left the room.

Dr. Burns opened up a cabinet, and took out a bottle of pills, marked Mifeprex RU-486. He opened the bottle, and took out three light yellow tablets. He handed them to Kiara.

"I take these pills now, take the red pill at home, and come back in a few days for a follow-up?" asked Kiara, her voice shuddering.

"Yes. As I explained, this is the mifepristone. It blocks

the hormone progesterone, which in turn will break down the lining of the uterus, ending the pregnancy. The misoprostol, which you will insert into your vagina at home, will induce the abortion, and cause the uterus to contract and empty. Within two days of that occurrence, come see me for a follow-up to make sure the abortion is complete."

"And this is definitely less painful than surgical abortion?" Kiara asked.

"It is, according to reputable studies and all of my patients," Dr. Burns ensured.

Kiara stared at the yellow tablets for a moment. She frowned. She, then, picked up her styrofoam cup, closed her eyes, and quickly took the pills, forcing them down her throat with the nasty-tasting tap water.

"Remember that once you take the misoprostol, you'll experience heavy bleeding within four hours, so don't be too alarmed. It's the pill doing its job," Dr. Burns added.

"Okay."

Nurse Carol walked back into the room with the signed consent form, and handed a copy to Kiara.

"Well, that's it for the visit unless you have any further questions."

"I don't have anymore questions."

The doctor walked over to Kiara, and rubbed her on the back. "You'll be fine. Don't worry about a thing."

"Thank you," mumbled Kiara.

"We'll leave you alone so you can get dressed."

Dr. Burns and Nurse Carol walked out of the room, and

closed the door behind them.

Kiara cupped her stomach with her hands, and started to cry.

✠

Gwendolyn and Reginald entered Nafiq's hospital room. The doctor, a young-looking Indian or Middle Eastern man, stood at Nafiq's side, examining him.

"Is he all right?" asked Gwendolyn.

"He has a Grade 3 concussion and a severe sprain in his left knee. I advise that he stay home for a couple weeks to rest and to immobilize his knee. I would also like to keep him overnight for observation."

Nafiq lay saddened as he listened to the doctor's words.

"I'll leave you alone now," the doctor said before he left the room.

Gwendolyn stood next to Nafiq at his bed. "How do you feel?"

"Horrible," murmured Nafiq. "I'm going to miss my game."

Reginald took a seat in a chair across from Nafiq's bed.

"That game should be the last thing on your mind. You could have been paralyzed."

Nafiq nodded.

Reginald continued. "I spoke with your coach, and he believes that your teammate intentionally tried to hurt you."

Nafiq was shocked. "Why? Who was it?"

"I was told his name is Michael," Reginald responded.

"Why would he try to hurt me?"

"Because you're gay," said Gwendolyn.

"What?" responded Nafiq.

"Although Michael isn't admitting to it, one of your other teammates heard him call you a faggot."

Nafiq was upset and angry.

"Well, if that's true, I'll deal with him when I get better."

"Nafiq, just let it be," said Gwendolyn.

"Let it be?"

"If you didn't participate in this lifestyle, then this wouldn't have happened," said Gwendolyn. "None of us would be going through this."

"So it's my fault?"

"Can't you see? God wants you to come to your senses. Doesn't this incident change the way you feel about homosexuality? Are you going to stop sinning now?"

"Please, leave," snapped Nafiq.

Nafiq instantly grabbed his head. It started throbbing.

"Please, leave," he repeated in pain.

Gwendolyn and Reginald got up and immediately left the room.

Tears filled Nafiq's eyes.

In the hallway, Reginald and Gwendolyn stood, talking.

"What are we going to do?" asked Gwendolyn.

"I don't want to talk about it," grunted Reginald.

Reginald and Gwendolyn walked down the hallway in silence.

CHAPTER 13

After a day and a half in the hospital, Nafiq was finally discharged. He left the hospital on crutches. Kiara escorted him to her car and opened the door for him. She grabbed his crutches, and he sat down in the car. Kiara put the crutches in the backseat, and got into the car.

"Do you want to stop anywhere before we go home?" Kiara asked.

"Naw. I'm cool," Nafiq responded.

Kiara pulled off, and headed to her apartment.

✠

In the living room, Nafiq sat on his sister's sofa with his legs propped up on the ottoman. Kiara walked into the room and handed Nafiq a glass of soda. She sat down in the chair next to the sofa.

"How does your knee feel?"

"It's sore, but it's not as bad as it was."

"Have you talked to your coach yet about your knee?"

"I called him today before I left the hospital. I told him that I wouldn't be playing in the game next week," said Nafiq, frowning.

"Don't be upset. You'll have other games. You know, everything happens for a reason."

Nafiq shook his head. "I guess."

Nafiq, then, lifted himself up a little to readjust his leg in a more comfortable position. He turned to face Kiara, again. "So how are you?"

"Better."

"Did you see a doctor? You looked like you were in a lot of pain a few days ago."

"Yeah. I'm fine. It was just fatigue. Nothing too serious."

Nafiq sighed in relief.

Kiara faintly smiled, trying to hold back her tears.

"Have you talked to Mom and Dad about you breaking up with Alonzo?"

"No. When that issue arises, I'll just tell them that we had different goals for the future and we couldn't compromise. That's all they need to know."

"I feel you."

Nafiq leaned back, and contemplated for a second.

"Sis?"

"Yeah."

"Does it bother you that you have a gay brother?"

"No."

"You're not embarrassed? You can be honest."

"No, I'm not embarrassed, threatened, or anything like that. We're all human beings, and we're all diverse. People need to stop wasting time and energy putting other people down. There's more important issues to address in this crazy world."

Nafiq smiled. "I'm lucky to have a sister like you. Thanks for having my back."

"You're welcome. And thank you for being supportive, too."

"No problem."

Kiara got up, and hugged Nafiq tightly.

CHAPTER 14

The high school gym was packed and noisy as cheerleaders rocked the game with their energetic, rhythmic cheers. Nafiq and his teammates ran out of the locker room onto the court right before the team from Simon Gratz High. Nafiq smiled, glad and thankful that he had recovered in time for the big game.

Julian sat in the bleachers by himself, waiting for the game to begin. He was very excited and happy.

Kiara sat in another section of the bleachers, snacking on a pretzel and anticipating the start of the game.

Gwendolyn and Reginald walked into the gym. Kiara spotted her parents, and waved her hands in the air, trying to get their attention. Gwendolyn and Reginald saw Kiara signaling, and traveled through the bleachers to sit with her. Kiara smiled, and gave her parents a hug.

"Where is Marcus?" Kiara asked.

"We tried to get him to come, but he refused," said Reginald.

Kiara frowned. "I'm sorry to hear that, but I'm glad you're both here. Fiq will be happy."

Gwendolyn and Reginald smiled, and took a seat.

Suddenly, the starting horn blared.

Nafiq, unburdened, worked hard, making three-pointers, creating his own shot, driving and dunking. The crowd cheered wildly as the Central star took over a very closely contested game.

By late in the fourth quarter, Nafiq had put together the game of his life- 31 points on 8-for-15 shooting (4-for-4 from three-point range), 11-for-11 from the line, 12 rebounds, 10 assists and 3 steals. But both teams were tied at 66 with only 10 seconds left.

Nafiq saved his fourth steal for the most opportune time. He jumped in front of the Gratz point guard, stole the inbound pass and started to dribble toward his team's basket. He could have dunked, but, instead, chose to fire a rainbow three-pointer from the top of the key. Swish!

A horn sounded, indicating the end of the game. The crowd jumped up, and loudly cheered.

Nafiq's teammates lifted him in the air, and paraded him across the court. Nafiq smiled, raising his arms triumphantly.

✠

Julian waited outside the gym locker room for Nafiq. Nafiq came out and walked up to Julian. They hugged.

"Congratulations. Wonderful game," said Julian.

"Thanks."

Julian smiled nervously.

"What's wrong?"

"I wanted to tell you something, but I'm getting butterflies now."

"Take a deep breath. Then, tell me."

Julian took a deep breath, and looked into Nafiq's eyes. Julian hesitated.

"You aight?"

"A little nervous."

Julian averted his eyes, and looked at Nafiq.

"I… I…" The words escaped Julian, again.

"You what?"

"I love you a lot."

Nafiq's eyes opened wide. He smiled.

"I've been wanting to tell you for awhile," Julian said.

Nafiq hugged Julian tightly. "I love you, too."

"I've never felt this strongly about someone before."

"I know what you mean," Nafiq said.

They both smiled and kissed.

Suddenly, a female voice shouted Nafiq's name from down the hallway. The voice echoed. Julian and Nafiq turned around. Kiara was walking toward them.

"Hey, sis," Nafiq greeted.

"Kiara, this is Julian. Julian, this is my sister," Nafiq introduced.

"Nice to meet you," said Julian.

"Likewise," said Kiara. "I've heard a lot about you."
Julian blushed.

"Are you ready?" Kiara asked Nafiq.

"Yeah."

"I'll call you tonight," Nafiq informed Julian.

"Okay," said Julian.

Nafiq gave Julian another big hug and a loving smile.

"Tomorrow night. It'll just be you and me," Nafiq said.

"That would be nice," Julian replied.

Nafiq and Kiara started to walk down the hallway.

"We need to stop and see Mom and Dad," said Kiara.

"Why?" asked Nafiq.

"They want to talk to you, again."

"Why? To tell me how I've been bound by some homosexual spirit, and that I'm going to burn in Hell, limb by limb?"

"Relax. I think they may be coming around finally."

Nafiq looked at Kiara with cynical eyes. "Yeah, right."

✠

Kiara and Nafiq arrived at the Johnson house. Nafiq rang the bell, and Marcus answered the door.

"Come in," Marcus instructed Kiara. He rolled his eyes at Nafiq.

Kiara and Nafiq followed Marcus into the living room where Reginald and Gwendolyn were already sitting. Kiara and Marcus took a seat on the sofa. Marcus folded his arms, wishing not to be present. Nafiq sat in the chair.

"Good game," Reginald told Nafiq. "I see Division I all the way."

"Thanks."

Reginald continued. "Your mother and I have been talking, and we would like for you to come back home to live."

Nafiq was shocked by his father's invitation. After absorbing his words, he smiled. "I'd love to come back home."

"This doesn't mean we condone your choice of lifestyle, but we will make a strong effort to accept you as you are. You're our son, and we love you."

Nafiq smiled, again.

"Great," said Kiara. "We can now resume being a family."

"Also, in honor of Nafiq's magnificent game, I've prepared a great feast. Let's eat," said Gwendolyn.

"That's what I'm talking about," Nafiq said, ecstatic.

EPILOGUE

It was the following year in late August. Nafiq sat on the bed in his college dorm room, unpacking his bag. He had just arrived on the Duke University campus. It was one week before the start of Fall classes. He opened up one of his duffle bags, and took out a few framed photographs. He looked at each photograph before putting them on his desk or bureau in his room:

Photograph 1: Nafiq stood proudly at his high school graduation. He held up a diploma in one hand and a letter in the other. The letter indicated that Nafiq had received a full academic and athletic scholarship to Duke University.

Photograph 2: Kiara and Raul (a.k.a. Investigator Martinez), her new boyfriend, posed lovingly together on a beach during their vacation in Puerto Rico.

Photograph 3: The Johnson family had a summer barbecue. They were laughing and appeared to be having a great time, but looks can sometimes be deceiving.

Although the tension between Nafiq and his parents had subsided, there were still issues. A month after Nafiq moved back home, he and his parents started to feud, especially when Nafiq invited Julian to the house. When they saw Julian and learned who he was, reality hit them hard. Reginald and Gwendolyn quickly reneged on their acceptance claim, and their relationship was filled with turmoil, again. Nafiq decided to live with Kiara until he moved to college.

Nafiq's relationship with Marcus was also filled with turmoil. Marcus refused to speak with Nafiq, and didn't attend Nafiq's high school graduation. Also, Marcus forbade Nafiq from attending his own graduation from UPenn.

Photograph 4: Nafiq and Julian sat on a bench in Central Park in New York City, smiling. Nafiq held up a Duke shirt, and Julian held up a NYU shirt. They were in love, and decided to maintain a long-distance relationship.

Nafiq smiled, and placed the photograph of him and

Julian on his desk. He then noticed an article on the cover of the *U.S. Weekly*, which had been left on his desk. Nafiq picked it up. The headline read: Super-producer Weds Into Music Empire Family. On the page, Alonzo and his new Caucasian bride posed for the camera at their opulent wedding. His new bride was the daughter of William Hoffman, one of the top powerhouse executives in the music industry. She wore a beautiful, Cinderella-like gown with a billowing train and a jeweled headpiece. The location and surroundings were also very lavish. Exquisite floral bouquets decorated the area. Businessmen and women, primarily white, congregated in the background, celebrating. It was certainly a fairy-tale occasion.

Nafiq frowned, and threw the newspaper into the trash. He got up, and looked out the window. It was sunny and bright. He thought about the past year and a half and how it was a struggle, but he successfully made it through. He persevered and also found true love. He breathed deeply, and though about his future. Nafiq was ready and anxious to embark on the next stage of his life- the college years.

BONUS STORY

RAIN

Short Fiction

It is 10:30 on a breezy, autumn night. Streaks of deep blue and black, with white sprinkles, are strewn across the sky. The marvelous light shines below upon Hassan's car, spotlighting his BMW with plush leather interior-- soft and smooth. ...Yeah. Soft and smooth like his cocoa skin.

Hassan pulls into a dirt path, behind a billboard, surrounded by weeds, bushes, and colossal trees. The leaves flutter to the ground, creating mirages in the night. He drives over broken beer bottles, cigarette butts, and newspaper remnants, searching for a secluded area. Coming here always reminds him of the mid-80s, of his high school days, when it all started. Those sweet, irreplaceable memories in his father's car, searching for that intimate connection that his girlfriends ceased to behold.

Hassan gets out of his car, and lights a cigarette. His light brown eyes glowing like a preying cat's-- like the flame he just lit. He opens his bottle of Bacardi rum...

At home, his wife, Olivia, tucks in their two twin daughters-- Angelique and Asante-- underneath their Barbie bed comforters. Their four-year old voices ask plaintively, "Where's Daddy, Mommy?"

Olivia responds in the most convincing voice, "He's working late again tonight. But he told me to give you two a kiss from him." Umm-wahhhk. Angelique and Asante smile, feeling complete again.

...Yeah. Hassan is always working late. Hard at work from 9 to 5 plus overtime, roaming the Acres. He's been all around town, and has no other place to go.

Throwing his bottle to the ground, Hassan begins his journey through the darkness of the woods...

The children have just fallen asleep. Olivia kisses their small foreheads, quietly shuts off the light, and closes the door. The hallway is dark, very dark, mars black. The light shining from her bedroom, down the other end of the hallway, guides her through the long tunnel, decorated with such paintings as Beauford Delaney and Lois Mailou Jones, and with cultural artifacts collected from, both she and Hassan's, travels.

Olivia enters the master suite, and frees herself of all of her clothing. Searching through the closet, she, finally, settles for her favorite, satin nightgown. She picks up the E. Lynn Harris novel that her best friend, Shanda, had lent her a few days ago. Slowly, she skims the pages before starting at page 1...

A tall, mysterious figure walks pass Hassan, eyes glowing. Hassan's heart starts pounding. Their eyes lock. The figure walks to Hassan, and begins to massage his crotch. Cold droplets of rain start to fall, emulating deep, Tribal rhythms. Each beat fierce and distinct. The figure stands back for a moment, admiring Hassan's body as if it were a Greek statue of antiquity. The figure, softly, whispers in Hassan's ears. "What do you like?"

Hassan, flush, thrusts the figure into him, touching his head. Umm, baby dreads just like his wife's. They taste each other's thick lips; they smell the dry rum on each other's breath. Hassan grabs onto the figure's throbbing manhood. Plunging deeper and deeper into ecstasy. Giving into each other's uncontrollable desires. Lecherous...

Olivia, already, on page 13, is no longer immersed in the novel. She's disturbed. Appalled. She slams the book shut. She has never thought about men and their secrets. Their secret lives. Those damn, reprehensible secrets.

The rain beats on the bedroom windows. Thunder rings. She gets up, and closes the curtains, hiding the rain running down the glass panes. Olivia feels humiliated as a woman. Angry. She wants to take them to court, get laws and ordinances passed. Punish them with the judicial system. She is ready to put her Harvard J.D. to action for the cause. Brothas like this shouldn't be tolerated...

Hassan notices the sun rising. The sky is painted with yellow, orange, and crimson chrome. He looks at his watch. It's 5:03. He was lost in another world. The world that is only true in fiction. Hassan hurries off, leaving his new acquaintance hanging.

Drenched in water, Hassan sneaks into the bedroom, and notices the novel on the bed. Skeptical.

Olivia asks, "What time did you get off?"

"About an hour ago," he sleepily replies.

The warm, morning sun shines through the curtains. The sky is clear. Hassan turns to hold Olivia.

"It was such a rainy night," mumbles Olivia.

Hassan replies. "That it was, baby…that it was…"